BELOW THE LINE

CONSUMERS UNION · MOUNT VERNON, NEW YORK

BELOW THE LINE

Living Poor in America

Photographs and Interviews by Eugene Richards

Text Editor: Christiane Bird · Story Researcher: Janine Altongy

For William F. Greene, Jr. 1945–1986

Library of Congress Cataloging-in-Publication Data
Richards, Eugene.
Below the line.
1. Poor—United States—Interviews. 2. United States
—Economic conditions—1981-   —Case studies.
3. United States—Social conditions—1980-   —Case
studies. I. Bird, Christiane. II. Altongy, Janine.
III. Title.
HC110.P6R52 1987   305.5'69'0973   86-70834
ISBN: 0-89043-061-6 Paperbound
ISBN: 0-89043-062-4 Hardbound

First Printing, June 1987
Printed and bound in the United States by
Meriden-Stinehour Press and Publishers Book Bindery

Rhoda H. Karpatkin, Executive Director, Consumers Union
Christopher J. Kuppig, Director, Consumer Reports Books
Nancy S. Miller, Acquisitions Editor, Consumer Reports Books
Meta A. Brophy, Editorial Production Manager, Consumer Reports Books

Below the Line was prepared for Consumer Reports Books by Eugene
Richards, Christiane Bird, Janine Altongy, and Nancy Miller. The book
was designed by Eugene Richards and Madalyn Hart. Carole Kismaric
was production adviser. Brian Young and Amy Whiteside processed the
film and made the prints. Additional research was provided by Hillary
Raskin and Megan Ratner.

As a courtesy, the names of certain individuals in *Below the Line* have
been changed.

Below the Line: Living Poor in America is a Consumer Reports Book
published by Consumers Union, the nonprofit organization that publishes *Consumer Reports*, the monthly magazine of test reports, product
Ratings, and buying guidance. Established in 1936, Consumers Union
is chartered under the Not-For-Profit Corporation Law of the State of
New York.

The purposes of Consumers Union, as stated in its charter, are to
provide consumers with information and counsel on consumer goods and
services, to give information on all matters relating to the expenditure of
the family income, and to initiate and to cooperate with individual and
group efforts seeking to create and maintain decent living standards.

Consumers Union derives its income solely from the sale of *Consumer
Reports* and other publications. In addition, expenses of occasional public
service efforts may be met, in part, by nonrestrictive, noncommercial
contributions, grants, and fees. Consumers Union accepts no advertising
or product samples and is not beholden in any way to any commercial
interest. Its Ratings and reports are solely for the use of the readers of its
publications. Neither the Ratings nor the reports nor any Consumers
Union publications, including this book, may be used in advertising
or for any commercial purpose. Consumers Union will take all steps
open to it to prevent such uses of its material, its name, or the name of
Consumer Reports.

Contents

Foreword

In autumn 1985, Consumers Union, which publishes *Consumer Reports* magazine, asked me if I would work on a book for them that would express something of what it means to be poor in America. As a photographer, pushed along by an activist past and an awareness of today's troubled economy, I wanted to be involved.

We began planning a book that would consist of photographs and taped interviews of the people I met as I traveled for several months across the country. We decided against a writer accompanying me, for fear that this person would be recording his or her own preconceptions, thus contributing to the stereotypes and generalities that are so often tossed about when poverty is discussed. People out there, we were certain, would want to tell their own stories, in their own ways.

To decide where I would go, who I would photograph and interview, we read news articles and sociology texts, studied maps and statistics and charts, searching for ways to address the issues of hunger, homelessness, and unemployment. We contacted social service organizations, public aid lawyers, and welfare departments to find families and individuals. Social workers and administrators were sometimes unwilling to refer us; appointments were broken. But finally our intentions were understood and commitments were made.

I traveled first out to South Dakota to spend time with the Timmermans, who were struggling to hold onto their heavily mortgaged farm. Then down to the border town of Brownsville, Texas, to see Mrs. Dolores Garcia and her children. Then to Philadelphia; to East Orange, New Jersey; to New York City; to Still House Hollow, Tennessee; to L.A.

As one person's history unfolded, I was often directed toward others. When I was with the farmers in South Dakota, who were threatened with the loss of their land and their way of life, I was moved to think of the migrant laborers who also work the land, yet have no title to it. The family I visited in the Tennessee mountains was barely hanging on in their ancestral homeland. How must it be then, for people newly arrived in this country, who must adapt to a new language, different customs, to an inhospitable economy? In Arkansas the children of the aging and weary sharecroppers I photographed could barely wait to get away from home. How much better or worse might it be for them in Chicago or New York?

From Chicago, I journeyed to Orrtanna, Pennsylvania; to Boston; to Douglas, Wyoming. I looked and listened. I came to know a few of the millions of people who live poor in America. This book, then, is the record of the places I went, of experiences shared, of the words spoken to me.

E.R.
January 1987

GANN VALLEY,
SOUTH DAKOTA

2

RALPH TIMMERMAN: Look. Jesus, look. Isn't this the most beautiful place? When I was a kid, twenty-five, maybe thirty years ago, I drove down here with my father, saw this land, and said to him, "I want this to be mine someday." And now it *is* mine.

Look at it! This is good farmland. Five hundred and eighty acres. And now they're gonna take it all away. How can you figure it? All these years we've worked the land and raised the food, and now Connie and me and the kids have to get food stamps to eat.

The price of cattle is down. The price of wheat is down. Can't get operating costs, can't pay for machinery. Can't even get insurance. How can you afford insurance? When you've got a steady income, you can do that. But when you don't . . .

We even tried breaking more land up to raise more grain. Mother—I call my wife Mother—about had a conniption. This land was native sod, virgin soil. A person lives here all their life, they don't want to see that stuff go under. Once you break the topsoil, it never prairies again. It's not money valuable, just in your heart.

We're $180,000, $160,000 in debt. It's amazing. When I started farming, if somebody had said to me I'd owe nearly $200,000 one day, I would have told them they were crazier than hell. I really would have. No way.

It's terrible what they're doing to us farmers. They're just doing it and it ain't ignorance, you can't tell me it's ignorance. 'Cause they're a hell of a lot smarter than that.

Nowadays, we live on just about nothing. There's no money coming in. None. Just the food stamps for Connie and me and our youngest daughter, Dawn, and some fuel assistance. Otherwise, we just do without.

We've worked so hard on this place. I'd give anything for this farm, anything. I even lost my arm out here. One night, about nine-thirty, I was driving the hay rack past a pile of old silage and manure and the damn rack got stuck. So I got down—the tractor was still running—reached way under and pulled the pin out. That was as far as I got. The damn thing went whoosh and pulled at me, took my overalls and started wrapping them up at 540 revolutions per minute. That sucker could have flipped me and killed me dead, just killed me dead. And then you know what? That guy above looked down at me and said, "One more chance." That damn engine died.

But my arm was still underneath there. I could feel my hand. I reached for my hand. I knew if I could get ahold of that damn hand, I could get the hell out of there, but I couldn't find it.

Our pickup was out here in the middle of the yard. I opened the door and the light inside went on. You ever been in a meat locker? You ever see what bone looks like when you scrape the meat off of it?

They buried that arm for me, Connie's dad and the sheriff. I told them to bury it deep, up in the cemetery in a Styrofoam box. So they dug it in and poured cement in it, with a little marker. The reason I did it that way was I had a friend that lost his leg and they just threw the damn thing in the garbage, and it started to hurt him. So, finally they buried the leg and that was the end of his pain. I don't want no pain, and I don't want some damn animal come and drag it off. Tough as I am, it'd be liable to die!

Back in 1973, I didn't owe nobody nothing. Period.

Then the fall come along and I wanted to buy sheep. But my loan officer down at the

bank, he said, "Naw, you can't buy no sheep. Sheep don't make you no money, no money at all. Buy cattle, you made a lot of money raising cattle."

I said, "Well, yeah, sure I did, but they ain't gonna make any money *this* year." He wouldn't listen to me. This idiot that don't know nothing. But okay, so hell, I'm gullible. I did what he said. I started buying the damn cattle. On contract. I bought four-hundred-some head—and I lost that money within six months. We lost every damn thing we had invested in the place, and ended up owing sixty to seventy thousand dollars to the bank besides. We had to take out a second mortgage on the house.

The market was just falling like crazy, and the bank wouldn't stand behind me. They wouldn't give me a guaranteed loan. So I got into FHA, Farmers Home Administration. They're supposed to be the lenders of last resort. Ha! The problem with these supervisors at FHA, they're young guys, just out of col-

lege, never did a damn day's work in their cotton pickin' life. Then they come out here and tell us farmers what to do.

They don't know a damn thing. I even went to the FHA back before I lost my arm 'cause Connie had had her pants taken off with that same machine that later got me. I knew there was something wrong with it and I told them I wanted to borrow money to get it fixed. I had the money there, it was money that could have been released to me. But they told me no! And we're supposed to listen to them. I don't listen to a one of them now.

All right. So that's '74. Then '75's not too bad. Along comes '76. That's a real doozy, a complete disaster. There was a drought that year. My corn grew less than half size, oats got dried out. Nobody had anything. I sold all my cows. I went and borrowed some more money, borrowed against the land.

Then I lost my damn arm. But the one that really put the nail in the coffin was an assistant supervisor with the FHA in '80 or '81. I

was raising pigs, about 35, 40 head. And this guy tells me, "If you increase these sows so much, you can make some more dollars, maybe pay these debts off." He said he'd worked it all out. So I bought more sows, 140 head. Then pyrovirus hits. It causes them to belly way down like they're gonna have babies and whoosh—no babies. They just dry up. They don't abort them, they just absorb them into their bodies. It hit all of them.

Now there's this letter. They sent it out about the first of December. It reads:

Dear Mr. & Mrs. Timmerman:

According to our records you agreed to pay $160,900.07, which includes various annual percentage rates under the Farmers Home Administration Indebtedness, on or before December 31, 1985.

Well, today's the thirtieth. We've got a day left, and I don't think we can dig it up in a day.

Me and Connie have talked some about filing bankruptcy, but we never done it. Bankruptcy ain't the answer. It's just a fast way, just a good sell-out process. There was a time when I felt bankruptcy was a way of surviving. You get to the point that the only thing you think of is how am I going to survive for the next round. But then we saw what was happening to other people. Everyone we knew who went and filed is gone now.

I'll tell you what, I've made my mistakes; Mother reminds me of that. There for awhile, I just felt like I failed. At nighttimes I would hardly get to sleep. Because I owed so much money to different people. But I ain't really failed. The system's failed me.

There's people in town that says the working class is subsidizing my life-style. The hell they are! I'm subsidizing them because the simple fact is when I grow wheat or corn, this place loses money. You know, back in '73, '74, we were getting about five dollars and something cents a bushel for wheat. You know what the hell we're getting for our wheat now? Three

fifty. And the same thing with beef. When I sell a beef for some fifty, say sixty cents a pound, when the damn thing costs me eighty cents a pound to produce, I'm losing two hundred dollars a head.

One guy said to me, "Don't you feel ashamed not paying no taxes?" You know what I asked him? "When was the last time you paid taxes?" "Oh," he said, "I paid them last year." I said, "I bet you tried like hell to get out of paying them." "Oh, yeah. Sure. I didn't want to pay no more than I had to." You know what I told him? "Hell," I said, "if I made the money, I'd pay it. I wouldn't even bat an eye. If I made $100,000 a year, hell, I'd be tickled to death to give it to Uncle Sam. 'Cause then I'd know I'd made a profit."

Hell, if we ever have to file bankruptcy, a Chapter 7, Connie and me and the family'll lose everything. We asked one lawyer how to figure what our house is worth and he said it's worth what it would bring at an auction sale during the worst blizzard of the year.

That same guy looked over our papers again and said, "You should file a Chapter 7. There's no way you can hang on out there." That was four years ago. I think we can hang on for at least two more years. Two for sure. Maybe three, maybe four, maybe five.

CONNIE TIMMERMAN: You know, to me this place is . . . this is . . . it's just a feeling. Even though by the time you've done lambing, and calfing, and planting the crop and harvesting, and all that, you are just so sick. But the next spring it's all new to you again—the oats coming up, or the wheat, or the corn. If we have to leave, it's going to be so sad. We kid ourselves and say, oh, it'll be a new life, it'll be fun, it'll be an adventure, but deep down . . . Our children grew up here. Carla—she's home now from college—she was a year old when we moved in, and our little one, Dawn, we brought her home to this house. Why, I even

remember coming here when I was just a baby. My dad's aunt lived here then and she had a lot of beautiful things. Oh, I thought this was the most beautiful house! The parlor had a sliding glass door and everything was just spotless. Glad she doesn't know how I keep it up.

We've had this land a long time. It's always been in the family. My great-grandparents owned it and then my dad's aunt owned it, and now us. That's the only people that have ever had the land. For over a hundred years. We even have a copy of the original patent on the land, signed by Benjamin Harrison.

You know, at least we aren't the first to fail, 'cause as the first, you feel like it's your fault, like it's totally your fault. But after all the bankruptcies and people leaving the land . . . Right in our neighborhood, you know, there are more and more people on food stamps. It used to be if you got food stamps, it was a rare case. But now, there's quite a few.

My theory is that there is somebody that wants control of the farms and the farmers, to control the food supply of the world. I look at that person as my mortal enemy, but I have no idea who it is. What is it that somebody said? You control the oil, you control the nation; you control the money, you control the world; but if you control the food, you control the people. And once you have the people under control, you've got it.

Could be they'll force us out and corporations will come in. But if it's going to come to that, food prices will be high. Don't kid yourself. They might be able to raise it a little cheaper, yeah, because they raise so much, but they aren't going to sell it at a loss like the farmers have been doing.

Guys like us, we've been through the wringer. We don't trust anyone anymore. Personally, I think financial advisors should be liable. Just like a doctor. If a doctor cuts the wrong things, he can get sued. What really made us angry was when we found out that Ralph could have got a five-year deferral on our loans when he got hurt. They implemented that FHA program but this guy that's

15

keeping our financial records down in Mitchell, he said to us, "I didn't know you guys were in trouble and needed it. You never asked."

God, I'd hate to live in town. Especially with Ralph's handicap. It'd be hard for him to get a job. I do think maybe he could get some training through the state, though. That would help. And maybe draw social security disability. There are some people who collect social security disability and don't work at all. But I wouldn't want to live like that. I guess I'd rather live out here not making any money than living like that.

I had to live in town once, for a few months back in 1976, and that was bad enough. I was thirty-two at the time. I had cancer of the cervix and had to have radiation therapy at a hospital in Minneapolis. We still had insurance then, thank goodness, and I had relatives I could stay with.

But anyway, while I was there, I met this one girl and she lived with her grandma. They had almost nothing, and yet they didn't dare leave their apartment unlocked. People would break in and steal what little they had. Imagine that! Out here, at least, what we've got is pretty well safe.

Ralph and I always say if we have to leave, we're going far away where nobody knows us. We say it, and yet I think it's just a big bluff. Come right down to it, we couldn't live where we don't know anybody. We've always known everybody. And everybody's known us since we were little kids. My parents live just a mile down the road and my grandparents, not quite a mile.

A family farm is more than just farming, you know. It's a way of life. It's not only what we do—it's what we are. And that's what's endangered here.

NORTH PHILADELPHIA,
PENNSYLVANIA

Francisco Gonzalez: Nobody knows me. Nobody calls me. Ain't have no letters for me. No have nothing for me. From nobody.

My mother ain't got nobody 'cause my father died. I no see my father. He died when I was a baby. He liked too much drink. Pain, here, in his side. Go to the hospital. Died.

I left Puerto Rico with my mother when I was twelve years. I live in California. I forget what city. My mother no working, I working. *Solo*. I make ten dollars. With ten dollars, you could buy food for all the month. Five bundle rice for twenty-five cents. Now, ten dollars . . . is nothing.

I no go to school, not here, not in Puerto Rico. There was trouble. I got hit on the head *cuando* baby. Special doctor checking me. The doctor say, "Maybe you no see no more. School no good for you." I say, "Okay." The water—coming the water from my eye.

I no read, I no write. *Ni* Spanish, *ni* English. Is hard. I get mad sometimes. Sometimes a letter coming here. I look, I don't understand. I put it down.

My mother died in '48. No, '51. I no remember. When my mother die, I no have nobody. I traveling with the car, working here, there, three or four month, moving all the time. Working in the factories. After California to Ohio, Florida, Virginia, California again, New Jersey. One time, I go in the car from California to Florida in seven day, seven night with a friend. I say, "Come on, let's go. I want to work."

I come here to Philadelphia in 1956. I like. I

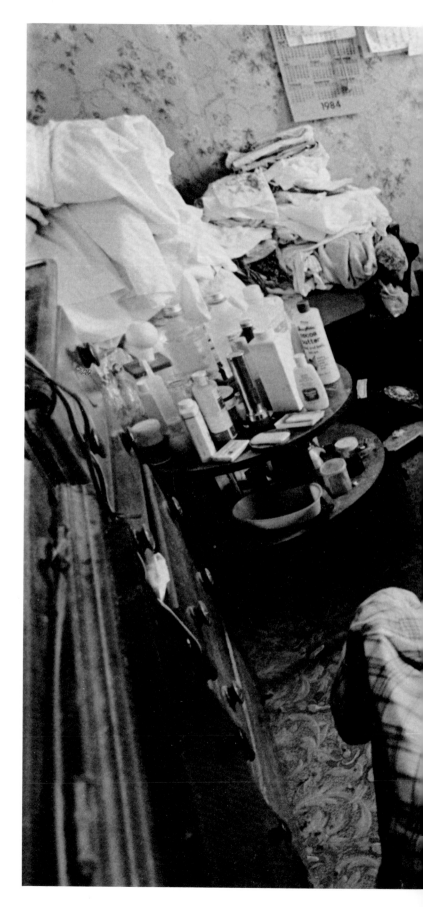

live in my car for two weeks. I had no place, no money. I park my Chevy on the street to sleep. Later, I sell it for a hundred dollars *para* eat.

I go to Mr. Chung for the cleaning, my clothes. He has laundry. He a friend. I ask if he has room for rent me, but he say no. Show me room down the street. I stay there. Then he move to this house. Then I move to this house in 1965. Mr. Chung very nice, Emily Chung very nice.

Mr. Chung died in this house. Sunday night he got pain in his chest. Monday morning, at ten after ten, he come and sit in a chair. Then he died right here, in my arms. Maybe heart attack, I no know. He young. *Como* sixty-two. I help with the funeral.

After he died, Emily, *ella*, no have nobody. *Ella* had one child, but it died, at three or four month. So she no have nobody. Just like me. I no marry. I no have nobody. No family. Only *ella*.

Ella no work after Mr. Chung died. *Ella* couldn't move, couldn't move her arm. She had the arthritis. She say, "I working." I say, "No, *ella* no working. I working. I working, you stay here, when I come here, you make my food, cleaning." *Ella* got nice for me, I got nice for *ella*.

When *ella* got pain, she tell me. She say, "I got pain here, in my leg." I rub her leg and it got better. When she got headache, same thing. All the same. She got same for me. When I got sick, *ella* call the doctor to the house. She pay twenty-five dollars. I no forget it.

I working many different jobs. I work at the coat factory on Second Street—jackets, everything for the ladies. I work there eight years. I no like. Too much trouble, too much heavy. I carry the bundles, seventy, ninety pounds. I carry on my back and I put it down. Heavy coats. Nine *horas* a day. Half hour for lunch.

One day, Emily here, we eating and boom, the seize. Trouble with my *corazón*, my heart. I go to the hospital thirty-one days. They put needles here, here, here, here. The doctor write the letter saying I quit work. But I no

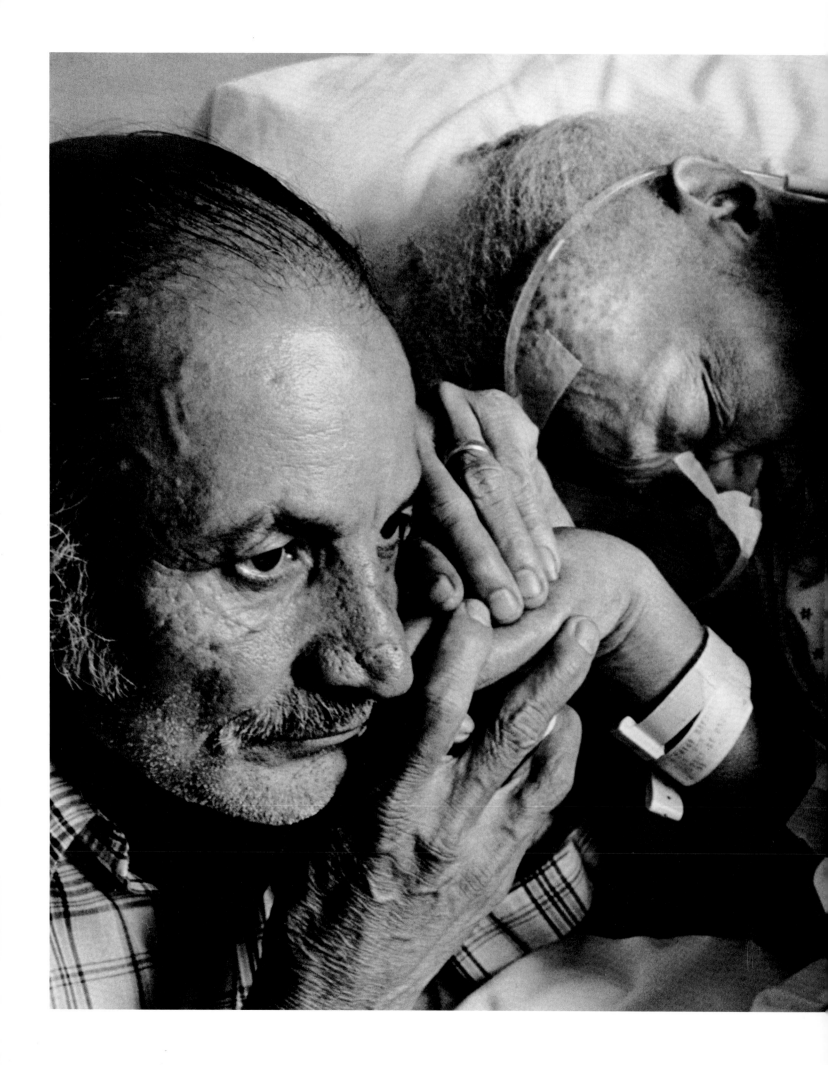

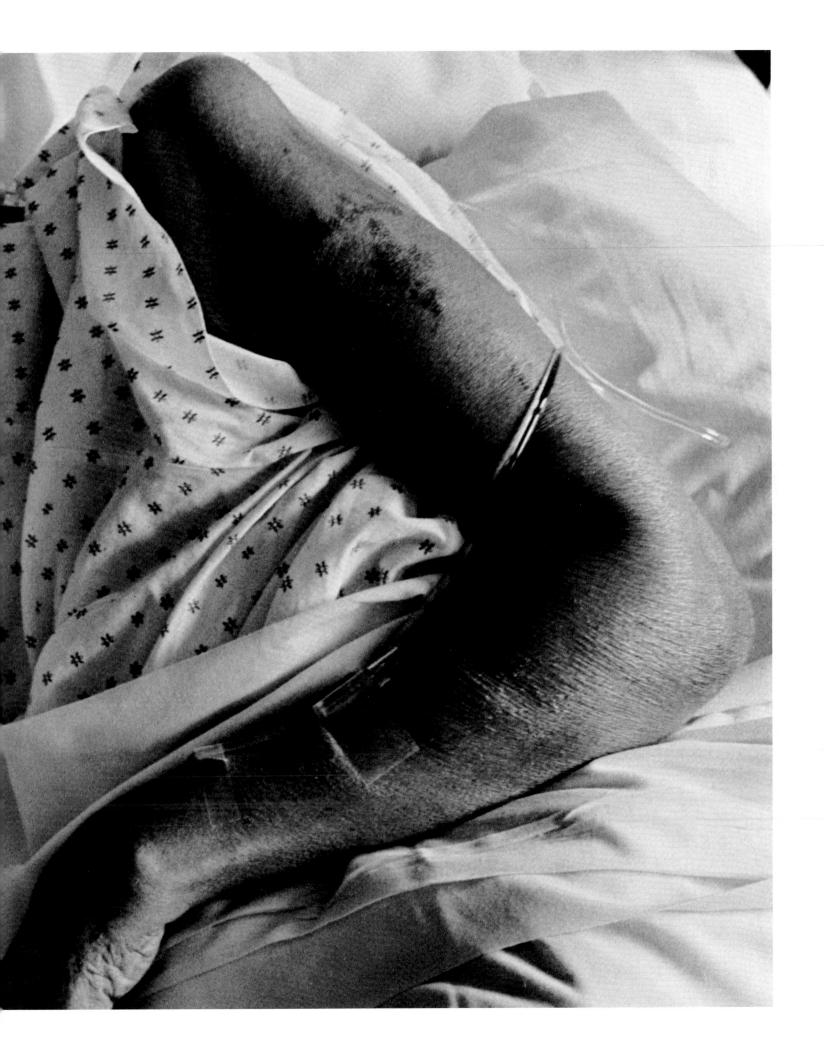

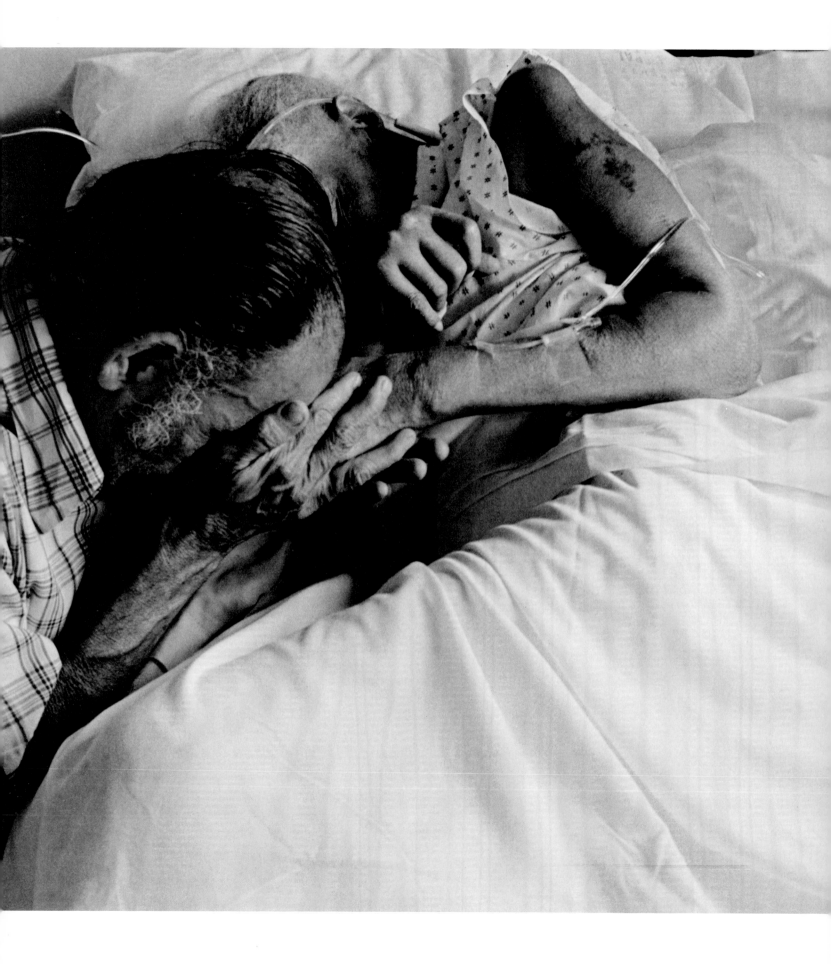

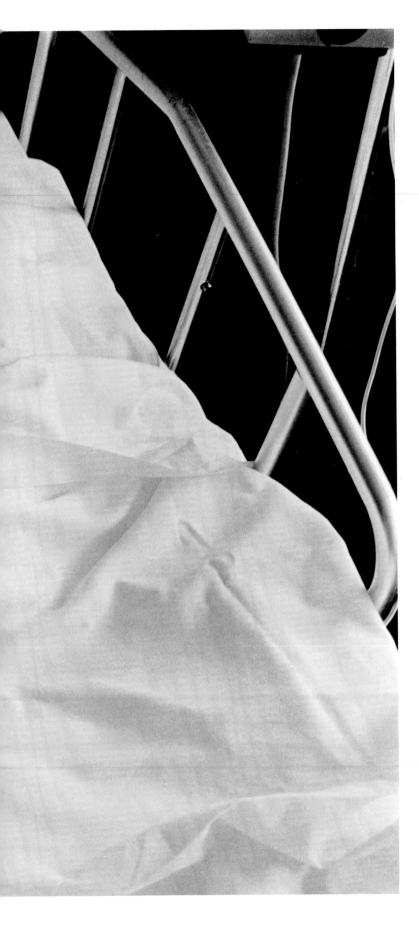

quit working. I get job working four hours a day, cleaning floors. Sometimes I make one hundred dollars a week, sometimes eighty, sometimes fifty. I got to work. I need money. I don't like to tell somebody, "You give me one dollar for cigarette, I give you one next time I see you." I don't like when nobody takes nothing. I like to work for what I eat.

One day I tell *ella*, "Mommy,"—I call her Mommy—"I sick. Call the factory. I no be working today." *Ella* call the factory. The factory say, "What? The guy sick?" She call the doctor. I got pneumonia. I got too hot, too cold. For one month. Then *ella* got the pneumonia. Two times. All the time trouble *y* trouble *y* trouble *y* trouble.

The union pay me when I got sick. *Compensación.* Two hundred dollars for two week. One hundred dollars a week. That's all right. *Ella* paid the Medicare. They pay for her. Now I don't work no more. I have eighteen, nineteen operations. One appendicitis, over here hernia. *Mucho* hernias.

I get money from the government. The third day of the month comes the check—$374 a month. I pay my bills. The house cost $150, the light $72, $75, the gas sometimes $300! That's too much, the bank checking. I got to keep my house. No eat, if no eat, but I got to keep my house. Mr. Chung, he give the house to Emily and me.

I got $10 in *cupón* for food for one month— $10. That's nothing. *Es loco!* Buys milk and coffee and maybe one bread. Milk buys $2, the coffee $5.95, the bread $1.05.

Now *ella* very sick. Go to hospital. No move, no open eyes. The priest come to hospital two times.

I visit *ella* every day. I get my visit at eleven o'clock. I come back, check my house about two o'clock. Then at three or four I go back to hospital. 'Til eight, nine. They very nice for me there. No trouble.

On Saturday, I give ice to *ella* and put it here. Put ice on her lips. She open her eyes and look at me. I say, "Mommy." I touch her hand.

I weigh 140 before she go to hospital. Now only 120. The nurses say, "You gotta eat, Mr. Gonzalez." I say, "Okay, I eat." But when I go home, I no cook, I go sleep. I ain't got nobody cooking. I eat maybe tomorrow morning. Same thing.

I stay all the time here, in my chair. Sometimes I afraid somebody come in, but nobody come in. I go to the store, church, hospital, then back here. I don't like to go in nobody's house.

I don't like the streets here no more. The people crazy, *la droga*—the drugs. Three, four months ago, bang, bang, shooting, killing one or two people. When my neighbors no see me, nine, ten o'clock at night, they bang on my window, boom boom, my door, to see I all right. They say, "Come on, come out, too hot." Forget it. Get out of here. I no bother nobody here.

I no trouble. I no drink. I drink coffee. I drink milk, soda, but no beer. Not me. I don't like it. I worked in the beer factory. Everything beer. I don't like beer no more.

I no watch TV no more. When *ella* in the house, she say, "Turn on the TV." She like it— the racing, the *campeón*, the fights. She say, "Look, look it, the fights, the fights." But now there's nobody here. I no like it, the TV.

Sometimes I forget things. Somebody telling me something today—they say I went to a tournament. I don't remember. I don't remember many things. I got a bump here. I was going down. I fell. I fall much. The seize.

Before, Emily found me. *Ella* watching *a mí*. Now nobody. I stay with Penny, my dog. *Tan chiquita*. A friend of mine he gave me. I no pay nothing. Now somebody say, "Sell me Penny, fifty dollars." I say no. I taking care of her. Penny eats everything. Rice, beans, everything.

When I hear the *música* outside, I close the window, I don't hear nothing. I don't like hear nothing. No TV, no *música*, no fighting, no radio. I don't like it—nothing. Only I like it the house. When Emily here in the house, everything all right.

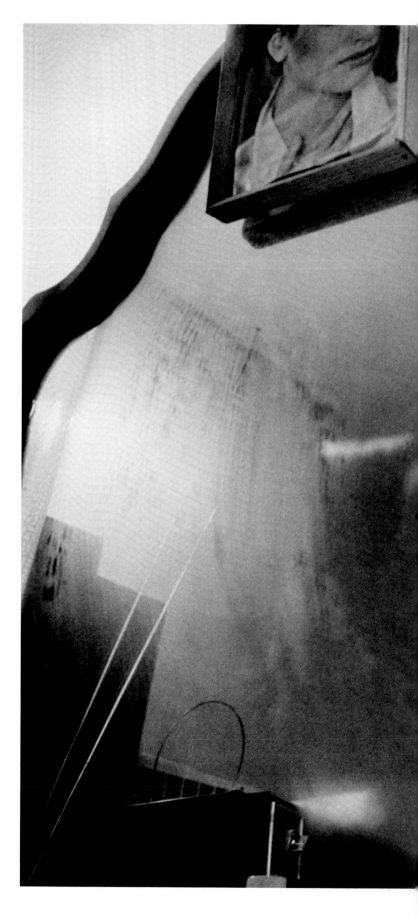

EAST ORANGE,
NEW JERSEY

JOYCE GRANDY: I used to cry a lot, especially when I was in my twenties. I was always depressed. I had beautiful little babies, children's kissing, I had everything. But nothing would make me happy. It was because I had lost Mother. I was just a little girl then. I was very, very close to her and nothing could take her place.

When she died, I couldn't believe it. It was like a dream. In fact, for all these years, until I met Jehovah, I couldn't accept it. Marriage never even helped it. That's why my husband Robert used to have so much trouble out of me. He would make over me so much and spoil me so much and I just, just would get really angry with him. Because it was really Mother that I missed.

Mother had patience. She taught me so nice and she never licked me. And she was so B-E-A-U-T-I-F-U-L! Beautiful appearance, beautiful figure, beautiful from her head to her toes, and beautiful heart. She was an usher in church. She was an Eastern Star. She was just a lovely person and quiet.

I always liked to please Mother. I had a big fat girlfriend, Ella Atkins, and my mother said she was so pretty and fat and round. And I wanted to please my mother so much that I almost prayed to God that I would get fat. Oh, Ella was so fat but she was so neat, and anything my mother thought was pretty, I thought was pretty.

So one day I looked in the mirror and I could see where I had got rounded and I didn't know whether I liked it that much. And my mother

said, "My goodness, you eat too much. You've got to stop it and cut down." She didn't like me heavy 'cause she had to make my dresses and it took more material, more money.

Where I live now, it's a boardinghouse. There's nine that lives here and some of the people don't have no sense, no sense at all! They're not crazy, just . . . off, you know, like that. When I'm home, mostly I stay in my room. I have my room on the second floor. They give you a bed with an old bumpy mattress and a chipped dresser. You can fix up your room anyway you like. I got mine with white curtains and a spread and all my shampoos and perfumes and things like that. I got a great big TV near the bed.

My room is so little. And it's always very, very hot. In the summertime, you know, the heat bites you bad. So sometimes I have to go downstairs.

Sometimes I'll stay down too long. Then all of a sudden, somebody'll bust out in a big argument and Barbara will start crying and Earl will start acting crazy and rolling his eyes and waving his hands. Then it will be too late for me to run upstairs because the commotion started. That's when my blood pressure will be dropped down and my blood be thin and I'll be so nervous.

When I first moved here and they used to have these attacks, I used to get frightened. I don't now because I've got used to it. They'd be carrying on so terrible. One night they sprayed roach spray on Barbara so she'd leave them alone.

We can't lock our doors here. It's against the rules and regulations of the Board of Health, 'cause this is a boardinghouse. So anybody can just walk in, just like that. Shirley comes in all the time. I don't like that. Shirley, she's Jamaican. She's the manager. She cooks our food and serves us our plates. She serves us macaroni and cheese or pork and beans. Sometimes a little piece of meat.

We all sit down and eat together. Shirley rings the bell. It's that jingling loud kind of noise, you know. It's like a jail house.

We have a schedule to use the bathroom. My time is eight o'clock, but it gets so busy in the morning. Oh my goodness. Everybody getting up, getting dressed. It's like a family, so noisy. Edna gets up at five. You can't sleep. So sometimes I wait and go in the bathroom later. I like to get fixed up nice.

If I wasn't here, I'd get about $210 a month on the welfare and maybe $75 in food stamps. But here, they pay *them*, not me. They give them the rent and the money for the food, which is $525. But if I was by myself, I wouldn't have that $525. I would only have $210. It's hard to get an apartment for $210.

I get fifty-three dollars for spending money. That's very little! Very little. I have to buy soap and toilet paper and clothes and things for my hair. I go to the Penny Pincher. And I make my own clothes.

What happened with my husband, Robert, is that he ran me down. He just ran me down to that point of to get married. I was eighteen and I had my oldest, Renee, when I was nine-

teen. Then I had three more—Debbie, Renault, and Katrina.

Robert worked as a cook for a time and then he came in making big money with the long-distance truck tractor trailer. He stayed in there. That's been about twenty-five years.

Robert was very smart and very, very clean. His toenails and his fingernails, he even kept them clean. He was a very hard-working person, a lot of talent, good-looking.

The way I came to leave him was when I became a Jehovah's Witness. I got an interest in that, and I got it alone and he got jealous of it. I'd seen his jealousy before, but not 'cause of religion. He'd be cooking cakes and pies and I would just get me a pickle and get my publication and read it and he would get in a rage because of the attention I gave my religion. It was like another man I was with.

So I left one morning when he went to work. He was nice, he kissed me, he left me coffee. It was heartbreaking to leave him but I said, "I cannot tolerate this."

After I left him was when I started on the
welfare. He didn't know it, 'cause he didn't like
welfare.

I had never knew about being on welfare
before and the little they gave me seemed like
a lot. I was young. Now I know it's not, but we
never went hungry. My landlady was a dear to
me—she was so nice—and Jehovah always
provided. It was always somebody giving us
something.

It wasn't hard raising the kids. Jehovah
made it very nice for me. They had socks,
ribbons, and their dresses so pretty, it was like
a little paradise. I always like little girls 'cause
they remind me of dolls and things. It was fun!

Robert kept asking me to come back. He
didn't like we was living poor. Not *real* poor,
but he liked us living up to the rates that he
worked, which was middle class. He didn't like
to see me on my own and he felt that I couldn't
take care of the kids and all that.

When Katrina got eighteen, I had to go to
the city welfare instead of the welfare for the
child support. I think that's when things
started getting tough for me. They just don't
give you enough. It's just not wholesome.

My childrens come to see me sometimes, but
not all that much. They're doing all right.
They have places to live, maybe not of their
own, but they have somewhere. Katrina is a
nurse in Tennessee. She got married and she
got a five-room apartment, so she has a beautiful life. I didn't go to the wedding because
it was in Tennessee. I don't have money to
travel with.

And Daddy, I lost him two years ago. My
sister had sent a telegram to Orange, instead
of East Orange, and they buried Daddy before
I ever got to see him put away. They didn't
have an open-casket funeral, it was closed.
That's the kind I say I'm gonna have. Maybe a
picture on it, but I just want it closed. Because
I think it's personal.

I want one of Jehovah's services with the
Kingdom records and one of them Brothers
giving the talk. Very simple and quick. I don't
want a lot said about me.

STILL HOUSE HOLLOW,
TENNESSEE

40

LETTA CASEY: We all call this place Rose's Creek but actually it isn't. Rose's Creek is where you turn off the main road to come into these mountains. This here's Varmint County. It's where all the varmints are from. And this little place is Still House Hollow. A hollow is a depression between two mountains. Usually got water down the center of it.

JR and me bought this little place here in the hollow for two thousand dollars. My uncle built it. It don't have no electricity and I don't particularly want it. The fact is, I was raised without it, but not my kids. See, I raised my kids in a town in Florida for a long time. We came back to these mountains five years ago. My children didn't know then what it was to raise a garden, to carry water, to light a light instead of pushing a button. They knew only one way of life and that was concrete. But I wanted them to know another way of life, the way I had growed up. Because it is here you can live when the big cities fail.

I never miss electricity, but then I never did care for television. The only thing I would say I'd like is a bathtub. I'd like that more than any of it.

Right now, we use an outhouse and we get our water from the spring. It's brown and gritty, but I don't think it's all that harmful. We keep things cold in the spring, too. They'll keep for a couple of days down there.

We raise a lot of our own food. And as far as gathering things out of the woods, the kids find quite a few things—walnuts and hickory nuts and little chuckleberries and blackber-

ries. So we don't usually go hungry. But there is hunger all over, and especially in Appalachia. I know it firsthand. I've seen too much of it. Maybe not so many babies dying of malnutrition, but still, hunger in the fact that people don't have a balanced diet and food stamps don't reach. No matter what might be said by some—they do not reach.

JR, he nightwatches, and there's two or three guys, no four, back in them mountains that works in a service station, and outside of that, I don't think there's a man around here working. At all. Unemployment must be close to 80 percent.

I went down to Washington to speak to the Select Committee on Hunger about that. I testified about unemployment, food stamps, generally rural life. The community developer here asked several women to go, but in the end, they all backed out. It's hard to go in front of people and talk. I went because I had my family behind me and it was something that needed to be done and I wanted to do it.

We had to go up to the table and just tell our own story in our own way, our own words . . .

I don't know what first brought my family to these parts but they've been here for some time. I was raised here, but back before we moved on into this hollow, me and JR and the kids was down in Florida for close to thirteen years. We were picking oranges and moving around. Then the money got harder to come by. The wages were cut a great deal from what they'd been and the price of food had doubled. It was just really hard to make it from one week to the next. So we came back here.

Now the kids know how to use a tiller, they can run a lawn mower, they can plant, they know everything they need to know to survive. We own this little acre and no landlord can come and say get out. Still, I never really know peace of mind because it does get rough.

See, progress has been slow around here. I would say that roads play a big part. They are treacherous, narrow, winding mountain roads—too narrow for the big rigs—and no

big company wants to be out in the boonies like this anyway. Small businesses, they're a possibility if some decision could be made as to what would work here, but really, ever since the mines went, we've had nothing around.

Some of the people have left. There was almost a total migration out of here after the coal ran out. But there's been a definite return. I think people figure in the long run they're better off at home. Here, there's always somebody they can fall back on. And then, too, people just naturally love where they've been born and raised. It's something I don't think any of us can really put behind us.

JR used to work in the mines back when he was real young and I was married to someone else. It was real dangerous working them mines. When they got in around the high walls especially. Or when they got a shot explosive loaded. Some of the mines were holes of water really. I can remember when I was real little, my uncle coming home with his pants legs frozen ice 'cause they didn't have a bathhouse or a place where the men could change or anything. So they'd come out of the mines soaking wet and they had to walk maybe ten, twelve, fifteen miles to get home.

I'd say most all the older men that worked in the deep mines, they got black lung. And cancer is pretty widespread around here. Emphysema too. I wonder about it. I don't think there's been any studies done, but there is a high cancer rate.

I've got cancer myself. It's in the cervix and both ovaries. I've been sick for awhile now. It started when we first came back here five years ago. I had got tired and wasn't getting along real good. Then we tried another child and it died and from there on my health just gradually kept on going down.

I'm in a lot of pain today. This morning was horrible to tell you the truth. It feels like fire more than anything. More of a burning pain. But if I'm sitting here and I'm crying and whining and really a moron about it, think how my kids are gonna feel. They're not gonna be laughing and playing and goofing

and wanting to tell me jokes and things. And to me, that's children.

Lots of times, I like to think about things from the past, those really happy times, wild and crazy, when we were younger and even some when we weren't so young. Stupid little things that maybe other people wouldn't even try to keep stored in their memory bank.

When I was born, they called me Doodlebug, I was so small. I only weighed about five pounds I guess it was, and all of Uncle Lee's grandchildren had been great big robust babies. So when he seen me and I was so little, he called me a doodlebug and everyone else did too. My uncle raised me. Mom and Dad never married and Dad was off up north. I never did see him. Mom stayed at Uncle Lee's too.

We lived about five miles from here, on back in the mountains, and it was a big farm compared to what we have here. We raised practically everything except our flour, coffee, sugar, and just a few items like that. I was a happy kid except for being an only child.

When we were fifteen, sixteen, me and my friends—JR and the rest of them—were all rowdy, really, a lot of times. I don't know how Mom stood us. All of us girls, we all had four or five boyfriends. I went with JR even back then and my best friend, she went with JR too.

JR was like most boys his age with nothing really to do. They worked during the week, stayed drunk all weekend. Drank, run up and down the roads, drive fast cars, that's about all they lived for. Everybody was into fast cars I think, back in the early sixties. I wasn't no different. I'm still a speed demon. I got one car that runs right close to 150. I used to have a Comet run faster than that. Helped build it up from stock. Run about 180. I used to run it up and down the interstate.

I went halfway through my third year of high school. Then I got pregnant, had a baby, and got married. I stayed married for a few years. But the marriage was no good, no good at all. And after awhile, I followed JR down to Florida.

I've had five children altogether. Some are grown and gone, but Henry Lee and J.J. still live here with me, and Charles, the oldest, is building his own house up on the hill with his new wife. Little J.J.'s real name is James Curtis. Junk-food Junkie, that's where the J.J. comes from. He's been the apple of the whole family. But they're all spoilt, more or less.

JR has petted them to death. There's not a one of them that don't know how to say, "Daddy, you know I love you," and get their way.

I've been very lucky to have met JR. We've had a lot of fun over the years. Things might have been rough, but we still had fun. But JR doesn't live here now. He had to move out so I'd be eligible for food stamps and a medical card. For me and Henry and J.J., we draw $153 on our check and $194 on food stamps. The main reason JR moved out, though, is the medical card. I couldn't get it if he was here.

See, we have a clinic here with physician's assistants and a doctor from Jellico that visits on Fridays. But the assistants can't prescribe anything really, just aspirin and such, and they kept wanting me to go in the hospital. I couldn't do it for a long time 'cause I didn't have no card or no insurance. So finally, when things got real bad, JR took off and I went and got the card.

That's when they did a D & C in Jellico and they sent me to Knoxville and they done a biopsy and started the radium treatments. I had an implant and more treatments and then another radium implant and then the rest of my treatments.

By the time I had got the card the cancer was too far advanced to operate or anything. They probably could've operated if I'd gone in earlier. But as it was . . .

The kids know I'm sick. They know exactly what it is and all about it. I wouldn't lie to them. Because I don't think it would be fair to say, hey, I'm gonna be fine, there's nothing wrong with me really. Because they'd know something was going on and they'd worry.

Maybe I'm more realistic than some. I accept

51

life a lot easier. I don't get as upset by it. Even through all the treatments and everything, I was basically happy. Even in the worst of times, I never did let things really, really get me down.

So many people, they get hurt or they get disillusioned and they just burrow in that thing, that's all they think about. I don't let myself get like that. I always start looking for something that has some sunshine to it, some meaning to it, something to look forward to. Even if it's only, hey, we're going swimming today.

JR WORLEY: I was named after my father, Henry Lee. Most everybody called me Junior as I was growing up and some of the kids hung JR on me, so I kind of went with JR.

I was born in 1945 in Kentucky, just across the mountains, but all of my family was from over in here. My dad was just over there work-

ing at the time. He never did work one place no more than maybe a year. He'd change jobs or the job would be run out, and he'd leave, go up north, find another job and then come back and get us and we'd all move up there until after awhile either he'd quit again or the job would run out and we'd move back.

I'm the oldest of nine. Mom more or less raised us by herself after her and Dad separated. Dad used to beat her a lot—he kicked and slapped all of us around—until she decided she couldn't take it no more.

I only went through sixth grade. I guess I didn't really get a chance at an education 'cause when you go from one school to another, this school's either ahead or behind the other, and after awhile you're so mixed up, you don't get the education you need. And then I had some trouble with a teacher. Come up over a fight and when the teacher started up behind the desk to get a paddle, I punched him.

After that, I left home. Threw my schoolbooks in the river, walked out on the road,

caught me a ride and went to Texas. On the road, you learn how to survive. Somebody's got a garden alongside the road, you take from it. That's why I always said I won't hurt nobody for going through the garden and getting something to eat.

After I left Texas, I went here, there. First time I went to Florida, I was working in a juice plant. I'd work sixteen hours a day and I managed to get drunk, catch enough sleep, and make it. I had a little girlfriend down there. When I left, I gave her my car, got me a fifth of whiskey, crawled on the bus and left.

I came back here. To sign up for the army. Then my cousin, he said, "Let's go up to Ohio, they're supposed to be hiring at a cannery." Why not? So we started running around, drinking, chasing girls, whatever. I've got a daughter from that time. I've seen her twice.

Me and Letta have been together seventeen, eighteen years now. She's thirty-nine now, but I knew her when she was three years old. We grew up in the same community. Her mother was sickly and I'd help them get coal and stuff. As a matter of fact, a number of times, I got them coal off the railroad yards, which is probably something a man can go to jail over.

So we've been friends a number of years. I'd come in every two weeks or so and we'd drag race. We weren't going together really for a long time, but I'd come down, pick her up, and we'd hunt us some cars to race and we'd go to a restaurant, get us something to eat.

One time, after I'd been away, I came back and found she had a baby and was married. She wouldn't tell who the father was and they was gonna take it away, so she said, "No, you're not gonna take my baby," and she got married. She was sixteen or seventeen.

The guy she married beat on her and the kid a lot. When I found out I said, "I don't want to interfere with your life, but my check's supposed to come to the post office here, you pick it up, sign it, and if you want it, you come on to Florida." So, 'cept for some small split-ups, we been together ever since.

We moved around a bit. Down in Florida, I

picked oranges, she picked oranges. I did some welding, mechanic work, whatever. For awhile, I got a truck and went to contracting. I'd contract a grove for so much a box of oranges and then I'd hire pickers and maybe I'd make a little extra off of them.

Then things started getting rough. It wasn't like it used to be, you couldn't just go to the grove and pick fruit. You had to have insurance, you had to have a license.

So we came on back up here. Up here, I've always made a job myself if I've made it at all. I hauled junk cars, worked as a carpenter. I even made moonshine for awhile, just like my grandfather, and hauled it up north. I never got busted. 'Round here, one neighbor just won't say nothing about the other neighbor.

Then, I got about twelve years in one of them big rigs, them tractor trailers. I'd drive all over the country, stopping back at home whenever I had a chance. I'd come in in my truck and get out and garden to put food on the table until dark and then I'd get me a few hours sleep and leave before daylight. Go on to New York City or wherever.

I'm not driving anymore. Now I work as a night watchman for a farmer. I make seventy dollars a week. I've always worked enough so my family has never gone hungry. We've got pretty close a few times but not that close. Not as close as when I was growing up.

Still, even back then I never really starved. I guess the only thing I ever hungered for was sweetening, but my kids have had it. I'd rather spend the money and see them eat it up, enjoying it, than run down there and buy something or pay to get my tooth pulled.

Me and the old lady never really had the money to have anything done with our teeth. Letta's lost all of hers. All of them. But even to get them pulled costs—well, the cheapest probably is ten bucks. Ten dollars will buy a lot of groceries.

So I've pulled most of mine myself. I've pulled all the bottom ones but three. Usually when I get an abscess on one of them, I'll keep

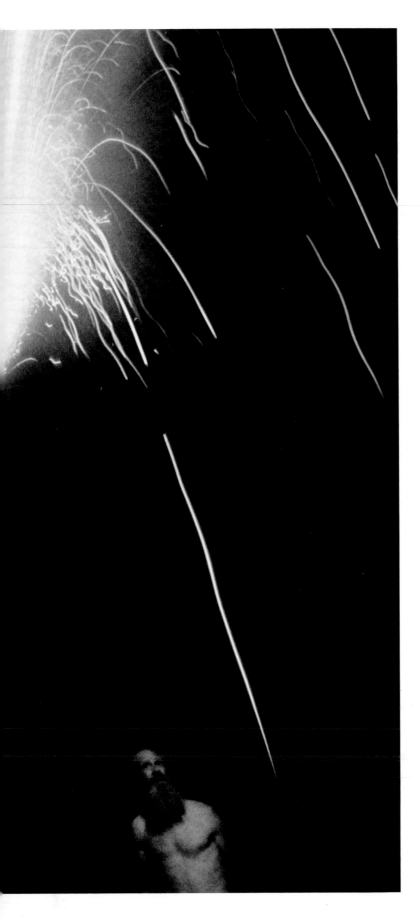

working it and I'll get it loosened up and then I'll tie something on it, give a sudden jerk, and be gone with it. As for infection, white oak bark, boil it and make a tea out of it, it's about the best thing there is.

Maybe some would call me a poor man, but it all depends on what you call poor. Poor as far as money-wise, maybe not having a lot of things that some people think you have to have or ought to have. But I'd say I'm a pretty rich person in my knowledge.

I don't want a whole lot. I just want my kids to fare good, to have clothes to wear, something to eat. I want them to be able to take care of themselves, and kill a deer or a squirrel or whatever it takes to survive.

I help the old lady and the kids out as much as I can even though I don't live here no more. I put the house in the old lady's name. It belongs to her and the kids. Still, I come over here all the time. I got a lot of work to do on the house. The roof leaks and I intend on having a generator, a pump, a bathroom. But you don't build it all overnight. I don't have the money. I may never have the money. That don't bother me. I can always load up the truck, stick the family in and leave. I'd find something, that's the way I've always been.

But the old lady's getting awful weak, with that cancer and all. She's gonna have to stay in one place. She needs treatments. Maybe she will get better, maybe she won't. I watched my mother die with it, I watched my first cousin die with it. I'll do whatever I can do.

She hurts a lot now. I've tried to get her to go to the doctor for two or three weeks now. The radiation left a lot of scar tissue and it's growing inside of her. She's a mess. I'd say they'll have to go in there and cut that out. I don't know if she'll go or not. Probably depends on how rough I get on her. If I throw me a fit, throw two or three things out in the yard and say, "Well, if you ain't going, I'm not coming back," then maybe she'll get up and go.

CHICAGO,
ILLINOIS

EMILY J. MARCELLUS: Where we live, it's like the dumps. I don't like the holes in the walls and the mouses. And I be hearing things on the back porch at night.

We got a stove, but our gas is turnt to the landlord and we can't get gas until he release it. And he don't. And in the wintertime, he only turn the heat up sometimes. Mostly it be like an air conditioner on. That's how cold it be.

The lights go out a lot. They been out for five days now. There ain't no bill due. The landlord, he just turn them out. He be playing with them. The lights go off, the lights come on.

I don't like the landlord. He think he bad. He be telling people where they can't sit. And he say you can't be drinking. You can't do *nothing* unless you gotta ask him. If you don't live here, you can't come around here, period.

In my family, there's me, my mother, my sister Shockey, my little sister Tika, my little brother Vernon, my little brother Cortez, my first baby Kenny, and my little baby Tequila. So there be eight of us here. And then when Shockey has her baby, they'll be nine.

Kenny's daddy don't act like he care about him. When he come over to see him, he be all mean. He's sixteen and he's dumb. He didn't finish school. He's in jail, probably. That's all he know how to do is go to jail. He a gang banger. He beat people up. The last time I seen him was Christmas. But Tequila's daddy, he come and get her almost every month and keep her a whole month. He tells me, "I don't want to see nobody else with my baby. Especially no boy."

Tequila's daddy ugly. He look like someone who did it and don't know what they did for. That's what he look like. I thought he was cute back then, but now I think he look like a black charcoal. He look like he all black. Just like my little sister Tika. We call her Blackie, 'cause she be all black, too.

The first time I was pregnant, when I was telling all my friends, nobody believed me. 'Cause out of the whole group, it was all of us screwing, they thought my friend Frieda was gonna get pregnant first. But I got pregnant first, she got pregnant second, and my other friend, she had a miscarriage. But she pregnant again.

They thought I wouldn't get pregnant first 'cause I wasn't that fast. They all used to just walk up to boys. I couldn't just walk up to no boy and ask them if they want to go with me. That's embarrassing.

I was scared to tell my mother I was pregnant. But she knowed. She just started knowing. I used to stay asleep, stay asleep. And then every morning I used to want Italian beef with mustard. So she knowed something was wrong with me. She said, "This girl eating like she's pregnant." And then I started craving. I started getting evil.

When she found out, she said, "Now what you gonna do? You're too young. You can't even take care of yourself. How you gonna take care of a baby?" I said, "I don't know." She said, "You want to adopt him? You want to give him away?" I said, "No, I don't want to give him away. I ain't gonna carry my baby for nine months and then give it away." "Well that's right. You ain't gonna give it away. You gonna suffer. Wait till it get big like you. You're gonna wish you never had no kids."

I used to run away, ever since I was twelve. I ran away after Kenny was born and I stayed away a whole year. My mother got custody of him. She said it was child neglect. She said I ran away and took him in one receiving blanket. I was telling the court I didn't, but they said they believed my mother. So she got him, until I get twenty.

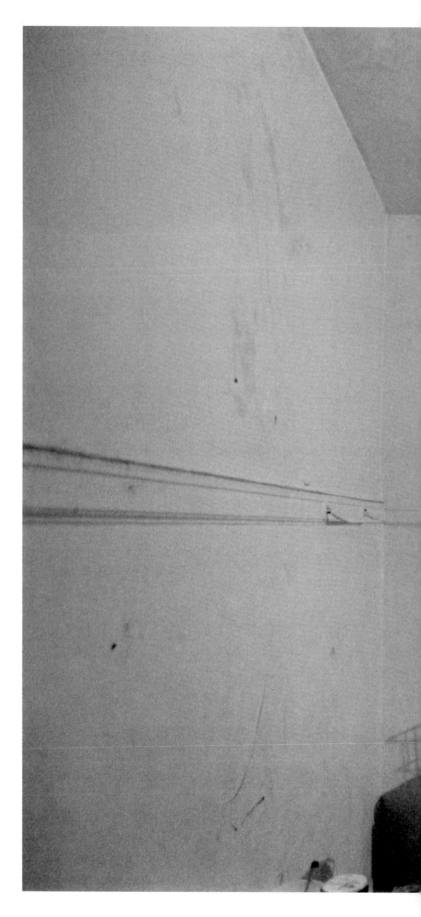

I came back when I got pregnant again. My mother said, "I knew you was coming back. And I knew why. I seen him, that boyfriend of yours. Every time he looked 'tween his legs, I knowed somebody was pregnant."

My boyfriend was gonna pay for me to have an abortion, but it was too late. I was three months and they say they wasn't gonna touch me with a ten foot pole 'cause I would've died, both of us would've died. See, she was breech. She had turned herself around. That's why it took me so long to go in labor. I was there six o'clock that morning and stayed till six that night. By six fifteen, her head was just out, but the rest of the body wouldn't come. Every time I tried to push, I'd just faint and woke back up. I looked like I saw the stars just in my eyes.

I hollered for pills. They wouldn't give me any. They say, "You a woman. You take it, you take it." I say, "No I'm not."

I was scared. I was crying 'cause my baby wouldn't come. They had to put one of those things 'round her head to pull her out, 'cause she was stuck. Then she just come on out. And the afterbirth was on her face. They had to put her in some kind of surgery or something. They say she could've died.

With the first baby, it was easy. I ain't have no pains with him. Well, one pain when I was at home. My mother was on the phone. I was just having labor pains, but I didn't know I was in labor. She said, "Walk around." And I fell to the floor. She said, "I know you're in labor now," so she called the ambulance. They took too long. She caught us a cab.

Now, I'm going back to school to the ninth grade, but when I make sixteen next year, I'm going to Job Corps. My mother's sending me there. She says she wants me to be a better girl than the rest of these girls out there.

At Job Corps, they train you in whatever you want to be. Nurses, doctors. Then when you get out, you can do what you want with your money. You can buy your baby stuff.

Me, I want to be a nurse. To show people

how it feel when they go in labor. To give 'em a pain pill.

I ain't gonna get pregnant no more. I got birth control. They gave me *strong* birth control pills. I ain't seen nobody with no birth control pills like these. I think they gave me *extra* strong.

No more babies. Having babies changed me. I used to keep everybody's kids, all my little brothers and sisters. I used to baby-sit, get paid doing hair, clean up people's houses when they go to work. But now I got kids, I don't do none of that stuff. I got lazy. 'Cause I wake up in the middle of the night trying to take Kenny to the bathroom and he don't pee. Then he'll lay right back down and pee in his bed. That is tiring. And I get mad.

If my mother don't watch them kids, I can't go to no parties. She be, "Where you figurin' to go?" I'll be, "To a party." "No you not. You're going nowhere and leave them with me." Now, if Kenny got Pampers, she'll watch him. But if he don't have Pampers, no, she ain't watchin' him.

I don't never want to get married. To nobody. Their daddies can keep in touch, but they better not ask me to marry them. I don't want no man beating me up. That's all they do.

See, I could beat up boys my own age, but I can't beat them big mens up. I'd have to run and call the police. My new boyfriend, Patrick, he don't beat me up. I beats him up. When he makes me mad, like when he gets drunk, I beat him up. He stays with me 'cause maybe he ain't got nothing else to do. Or 'cause maybe he be scared of me. 'Cause he says, "If I quit you, you're gonna kill me."

I don't like mens. Some men like taking your money. Some like beating you up *and* taking your money. It happened to my mother. She used to buy her husband fifty-dollar pants and he still took her money. She used to go to the fashion hat store and buy him a hat that cost sixty-five dollars and he still take her money. Then she bought him a rabbit coat cost three hundred dollars. And guess what he did with it. Gave it to his girlfriend while she was on her period and *laid* on it.

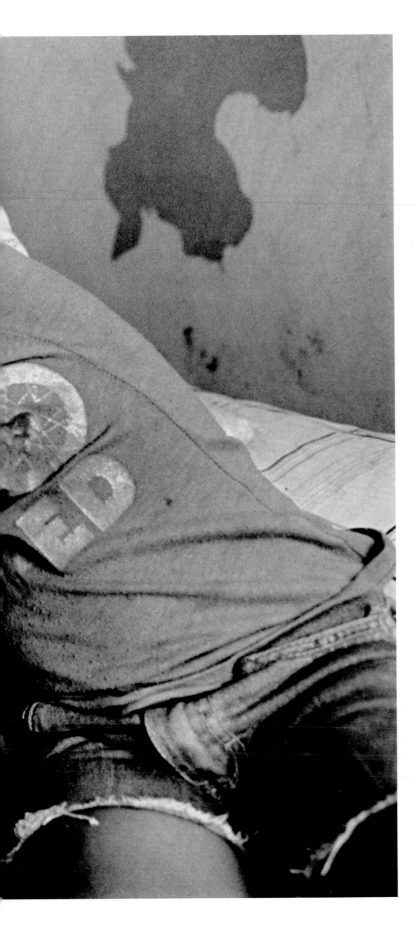

Once he tried to whup me, so I tried to burn him. I told him, "You ain't my daddy. Don't try to whup me or I'll kill you." He and my mother got a divorce 'cause he thought I was crazy. Then my mother took me to a psychiatrist and he said I was a little off balance. I don't know why. I ain't crazy. I have good sense.

CHUCK LONG: Emily! Emily seems young. Yeah, she does. Shockey's only thirteen, but she seems more mature than Emily. Emily might be kind of slow. She might have a lot of problems when she a little bit older. Emily, she don't know—she don't know what she really want out of life.

Me, I want to have a good job, a house, and a family to raise, you know. I want to get married. I got two families. I want to have a house for one family; for me and Shockey and the baby she about to have. My other baby can always come and spend nights with me. But not the mother!

I got one son. He's just seven months. His mother's seventeen now. She was sixteen then. We was together, but we broke up, really. Then we made love and she got pregnant. First I didn't believe it was mines. I asked for a blood test. I had to, when she told me she laid with somebody else. Turned out it had my blood, so from that day on I been taking care of it. I receive a little check. A general assistance check. And I do what I can with that. But it ain't doing too much 'cause $154 ain't no money.

This second baby was a shock to me. I was just in a trance when Shockey said she was pregnant. I was like, "What?" And she just told me she wanted it. I kept asking her, "You sure you want this baby? You wanna go through with this?" She tells me, "Yeah, I wanna have the baby." So then now, today, she asks me, "How you gonna take care of me and the baby and plus you already got a baby?" I said, "I don't know." Which I don't. I tells her I gotta get out and get a job, but I know it ain't

gonna be that easy. And she just said, "Well, I hope you get one." I don't hope. I wish for jobs. I pray for them. 'Cause see, jobs just don't want me. I've lost so many jobs, it's a shame now. They'll tell me, "We lost your application," or something like that.

Lots of men, they don't want nothing to do with their babies. I just can't see myself doing that, 'cause when I'm devoted to somebody, I'm gonna stick with them. I look at it like, she got pregnant by me, so I gotta take care of that.

Things are different since I've had my babies. I don't do as much as I used to. I don't hang out as much. I used to keep my little reefer and keep my beer. I used to drink beer all the time. I don't do that no more. I do it once in a while. And I don't buy reefer no more, it's too high. Twenty-five dollars for six joints or twelve to thirteen dollars for four.

I used to gamble, too. Either shooting dice or playing basketball for money. But I had to stop, 'cause my luck was going bad. I lost ninety bucks shooting dice. And I was sup-

posed of been coming here to take Shockey out. I thought I'd win more money trying to impress her, you know.

Most of my friends been in trouble. Most of them been in the Home three years straight, five years straight. Now they doing time in jail. I got four friends in jail right now. Attempted burglar, murder, robbery. I ain't never did none of that. It never crossed my mind to do it. I got high a few times and got disorderly, but I ain't gonna be going through all that frustration, worry about the police and stuff.

Marriage? I thought about it, but I don't think Shockey's gonna be willing to go through with no marriage. I talk to her about it and I tell her, "Well, you're just thirteen. And I'm twenty. So don't just set your little heart on me. 'Cause you're really too young to be talking about love, anyway."

I didn't know how old Shockey was when I first did it. I ain't asked her. I thought she was about seventeen, 'cause I looked at that body

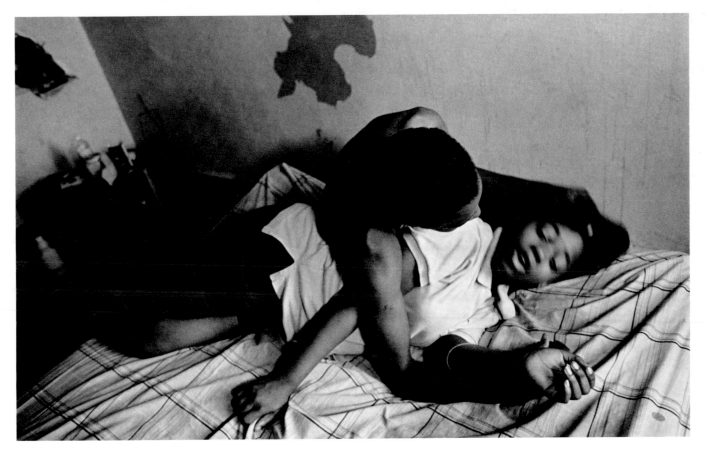

74

and it was like "Wow." Peaches was the one that told me her age. Peaches, that's what I call Shockey's mother. It's a nickname, I guess. Anyway, I was like, "What? You twelve? You didn't tell me that. I could be in jail for statutory rape. That's the first thing a judge's gonna look at is our age difference."

When I'd be telling all my friends, "Yeah, she's just thirteen," they'd be telling me, "Then just leave her alone, child molester," you know. But I'd be telling them, "It's not that easy, 'cause being with her for so many months, I got feelings for her."

I'm crazy about her. I tell her if I could find a job, she could've been moved out of this place. I had moved one time, 'cause me and my mom wasn't getting along that tough. And I told Shockey she can come with me. So Shockey got her clothes and was staying with me. And the next day when we came around here, her mother say, "Shockey, you gotta come upstairs at ten." And I was like, "Well, but she's staying with me." She said, "No. She gotta come home, otherwise I'm gonna put out a missing." I said, "Well, okay." I kissed her good night and everything. And then her mother asked me to come back and live with them. 'Cause I do a lot around here. If the janitors can't do it, then I'm gonna do it. Like that sink in there. I'll fix the sink. And the lights. Hook them up to the outside.

Yeah, this place is a dump. That hole in the kitchen? One Sunday we was cooking dinner and the wall just fell right into the pot. And that's when the roaches started coming in. And the waterbugs, and the spiders, and the mices. I mean, we got more mice and roaches than a alley.

This is a condemned building, if you ask me. Or it should be, 'cause in the winter, there wasn't no heat. I had to go get plastic and put it in every room in the house, 'cause with the holes in the wall, you could feel the breezes coming through. Little Kenny, Emily's baby, he stayed in the hospital, I'd say from January 'til about March. He's got asthma, you know. He got too sick in this apartment.

There be burglaries in this building. Something like every two weeks, you know. Lady across the hall, her house got broken into. And then there's dope dealers in back. Kids can't even go out and play without the dope dealers flashing their guns.

You walk around here late at night, you're lucky to survive. They raped a woman about a month ago, right in front of this building. And everybody, you know, neighbors, looking out the windows, and nobody don't call the police.

I was watching from my window, Emily and me. I see this man on top of her, rolling her. And then two more guys come from around the back. When they got through, they just left her laying there.

The lady was kind of young, about in her thirties. They gave her some type of drug 'cause she could hardly stand. She came crawling up here, knocking on the door, no clothes on. "Help me," like that. I wanted to open the door but I didn't.

There's a lot of cops around here now 'cause somebody tried to set this building on fire. It happened about two weeks ago. Somebody threw a cocktail or whatever you call it. Put a towel in a glass with some gasoline and lit it, and threw it against our door. The whole thing was in flames. Everybody was sleeping and smoke was through the whole house. My brother, he woke everybody up. We had to keep throwing water on it and it took about a half hour to put the fire out.

It could've been the landlord that done that, 'cause he's the one that burnt down the first half of this building. I guess he did it for insurance.

If Peaches's place was burnt, she could've been got out of this dump. Peaches looks depressed. She is depressed. She got one daughter with two kids. She got one daughter with one on the way. And she got all those other kids. And they all been having a hard life. It's even harder now that they staying in this building. See, by the wintertime, it's gonna be rough. Even more babies gonna be in this house.

ORRTANNA,
PENNSYLVANIA

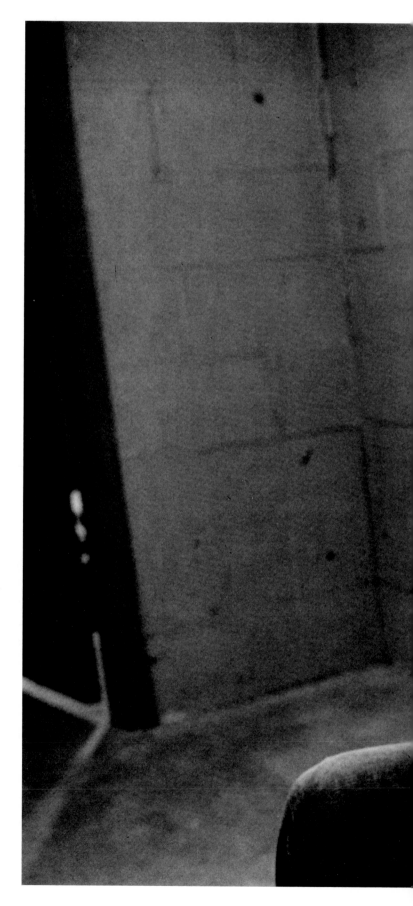

SAMUEL JENKINS: I've been a migrant worker for umm, between fifteen, seventeen years. No one ever pays attention to migrants. We don't rate as important.

I'm forty-one, from Richmond, Virginia. I've got five sisters and three brothers. My father was a self-employed landscaper, come out of South Carolina. My mother was from Magnolia, North Carolina. And they're somewhat country style, a church family. They raised us up in the city sort of old fashion. We got whuppings for doing the wrong thing and not being respectful to people and not following rules.

I completed the ninth grade, on the honor roll. Except in conduct. Throwing spitballs and shooting bean shooter at a guy with a bald head.

I used to lift a lot of weights. At the age of fourteen I was about 185, 190 pounds, and played football real good. I played good guard, tackle, linebacker. I went to school with Willie Lanier who became the linebacker for the Kansas City Chiefs and another guy who played for the Milwaukee Bucks. I more likely would have went pro myself.

But I dropped out. 'Cause I took to the street and got into hustling. Selling reefer, safe cracking, breaking and entering. I ran around with older guys. They were anxious to teach you things like that. I didn't need the money. I could have gotten that at home. But I heard, "Well, you're chicken if you can't do certain things." So to prove myself on the streets I showed I could do just as good as the rest.

I served a little time. The charges against

me were breaking and entering, street fighting. The first time, they gave me two years. I went in about seventeen, and did time on the chain gang road camp, cutting right away, digging ditches, sometimes breaking ice up in fourteen-degree weather.

When I got out at nineteen, I got into more trouble. Same thing, breaking and entering. I did four years, eight months. The third time, I did eight months. Then I came on back to Richmond. I wasn't twenty-five yet, and I was approached regular by the police every time I was seen. I was just harassed, stopped, and anything that happened I had to be the one that did it—so I went on to Florida and I went to the woods. I had my little homemade tent. I'd come out every now and then to pick oranges to eat. Otherwise I'd just stay in the woods. My family didn't hear anything from me 'til about seven years. I just didn't communicate.

I chose another name in the wilderness. Allan Freeman Life. It's a spiritual name, just something dealing with the infinite source. Like "Allan," that's "A-L-L," the all, even though the "A-N" is on it. And "Free Man." Then "Life," dealing with my new way of life.

I'm not a Rasta, not in the organization or any cult, but I let my hair grow in the wilderness, 'cause everything around me grew natural as it was. A lot of people make fun of it. Had I gotten a haircut, I wouldn't see life from the angle that I can see it from now.

After those seven years, it was time for me to come out of there. So I came out. And I came out a different person than I went in. Through my once complicated mind, I could see things in a more plain and simple way.

I went back home and regrouped with the family. And we got together and we started singing like we always did. And we would have fun and I'd be there for awhile and I said, "Well, I'm going on." "You're going again?" they asked. "Yeah, I'm going."

I got into the migrant thing. It was kind of interesting to me. A migrant is a person that goes from place to place to harvest crop.

My first migrant job was picking oranges in Loxahatchee, Florida. And from then on, I got to drift about according to where I heard the best crop was. And once the season would wind up in Florida, I would follow it to the other places—North Carolina, Virginia, New Jersey, Pennsylvania—where they would go picking apples or cucumbers or peppers.

Most interesting were watermelons. When I first got into watermelons, it wasn't like work. I was being a weight lifter, I was just having fun, making money having fun because there was a lot of exercise involved in it. But after getting into it awhile, I seen it was different.

They say picking's unskilled, but you have to be really skilled to pick. When I first started picking oranges, it was hard on me because I didn't really know how to handle the sack. I would carry the sack on my shoulder but I learned later that I should rest it on the steps of the ladder, because a sack of oranges weigh from about 96 to 120 pounds.

When I first started, we made, on average, from fifty to sixty cents a box for big oranges. And for seventeen years, it's been the same thing. Now you get sixty-five cents.

Recently, most years, I've made between $2,000 and $2,500. So if it wasn't for food stamps and the missions that donate clothes or something every now and then, it would be kind of rough. But I don't want to feel like a cripple. I don't want to depend on food stamps. I want to work and make a decent wage.

Migrants have no health insurance, but we have access to the clinic. In some states they have vans that carry you back and forth, but in some states you don't. So sometimes it's just not that easy to get to these places. You know we people oftentimes get sick. No one can definitely say it can be from the poisons on the trees, and no one can say that it's not. I believe it's a danger. We work around chemicals regular. Especially in the orange grove. A lot of times I work in the orange grove a week's time, and when I blow my nose, I don't know what it be. It be black.

The most I ever made was $133 in one day.

That was loading watermelon. And I've had a solid week of making $100 or more in watermelons. During that time, I saved money. I had my apartment. Everywhere I went I had my apartment and I could afford to get me a TV, a radio, or the things I wanted. I haven't had a good season since then. It's just been freezes hitting Florida back to back. When I first went there you could pick a bin of oranges on one tree. But now you pick sometimes four or five trees on the average to get a bin.

Then there are many more people picking. 'Cause there are a lot more immigrants. Haitians. Puerto Ricans. Mexicans.

You know, I like to see people work if people need work, but Haitians got a lot of privileges, better privileges than Americans. See, an American will go to the bus when they're loading up and ask for work and they'll tell him they don't need anyone. Then they'll go and hire the Haitian 'cause he'll work for their prices. An American will want a fair price, so it's hard for him to get work. I mean, I'm a

citizen in this country. I need to pay rent too.

To keep out of debt, I've got to make at least minimum. That's three thirty-five an hour. But then the minimum don't really happen in some places. Like I went to North Carolina. I get a job working in some pickles, and I pick all day long. But the fields have already been picked three or four times so I don't get that much. I only make nine to twelve dollars in a nine-hour day. So then, they give me a receipt that say I only worked two or three hours instead of nine to match it up with the minimum wage.

Most migrants work with contractors. Most of the contractors that bring the guys up from Florida, they're black. The farmers are mostly white. The contractors get the migrants for the farmers. Now, anywhere I'd be working for a contractor, I wouldn't be making, say, twelve dollars for a bin of apples, I'd be making eight, while the contractor be making four. Only thing he do is bring the workers up here in a van, keep them in order. And he's making four

dollars a bin, per person. So if he's got twenty people picking, he can make out pretty good.

Many contractors, they bring the guys up early, to get them in debt first. You have to depend upon living in a motel—eighteen dollars and up a night. Then you got to buy the food from the contractor, forty dollars a week. He makes his wife—they always bring their wives—do the cooking, and we got to buy their food, whether we eat it or not. Every now and then you find some that let you buy your own food. But they takes the kitchen, they takes the stove. Most times, too, we can't go shopping 'cause we're not near a town. We don't have transportation.

Last year I left Belle Glade, Florida, and I was told I could make fifty dollars a day picking corn up north. And we would have eight solid weeks of work. But when I got there, I sat around might near two weeks before I got a first day of work. I had a food bill and I had a rent bill. So I started working, the contractor deducted everything and left me a balance

due. And every time I make some money, I owed it. And it's been like that every time. For the last four or five years.

The contractors got henchmen, most of them. Two or three guys that they'll rough people up with. They got their ways of threatening. Guys are actually afraid to walk off a camp, camps that could be considered slave camps, 'cause they live in fear. Some of the things I been witness to—I see people pistol-whipped, shot. I seen a man getting hit in the head with a tire iron. I tried to get the man to complain about it, but he was too afraid.

I have a book, a book for migrants entitled *Know Your Rights*. I studied it and I see a lot of violations around. I know anyone can make a mistake, but when I see a person going to an unnecessary limit just to push over, bully people, then I feel that I have an obligation to the Creator and it's time to complain.

It's risky, but I just feel like there's some spiritual force that's kind of helping me through, 'cause there's been some close situa-

tions for me. There have been several contractors that really wanted to jump on me, for interfering with advising workers of their rights. They come to approach me, "Well, I can't have you telling me how to run my camp." And they be whispering amongst each other. One of them had picked up a two-by-four. One reached and put his coat back and let me see his pistol. But for some reason I was spared. They didn't follow it through.

I've been involved in some suits against this one contractor. He didn't pay me what I was supposed to make. We started about seven thirty that morning and I worked 'til a quarter past six that evening. No lunch. And I made twenty-five dollars, not even the minimum. Then he took four dollars out of the twenty-five for social security. You don't take four dollars out of twenty-five.

The legal aid, they tell the migrants, "We're here to help you. If anything happens, if any of your rights are violated, come to a phone and call us secretly and we'll take it from there." So I did. And this contractor went to court. They found him guilty.

Right now, I'm not working for a contractor, I'm working for Mr. Woerner. This is the first time I've been hired directly by a farmer and he's a fair person. He pays four dollars an hour until piecework begin. Today I made thirty-six dollars.

Mr. Woerner is the type of farmer that gets right out and works with the migrants. Very few will do that. Most of them just ride around in pickup trucks all day and just exercise their powers. Most of them see migrant workers as what they normally call us, season tramps. They often say all we need is a bottle of wine and something to eat.

The public eye don't see the way of the migrant. They don't see the pressure that we're going through. I can't stand it really. 'Cause we have worked too hard to be confronted with being brutalized . . .

There's nothing in the future really for the migrant. That's why he has no ambition. He looks ahead of him and he sees only a cloud.

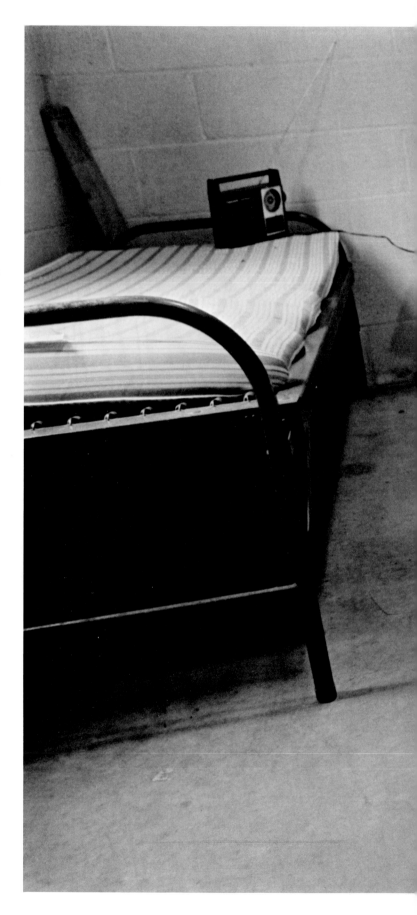

DOUGLAS,
WYOMING

CONNIE ARTHUR: I get my schedule from Safeway on Fridays, and you might say my life
goes according to that schedule. I plan my
other jobs around it.

So if on a Tuesday I have to be at Safeway at
4:00 in the morning, I get up at 2:00 A.M.—
earlier when the roads freeze and it's twenty,
thirty below—do the paper route for the
Casper Tribune, which is about eighty-five papers, then go to the store, stock shelves. Take
off at 6 A.M. on my lunch-hour break and do
the *USA Today* papers. Then clock back in at
Safeway and work until 10:00. Take a fifteen-
minute coffee break and then work 'til 1:00
P.M. Then go to the Country Inn to clean until
2:00. It's mostly do the kitchen floor, the
bathrooms, vacuum, wash the windows. All in
all, that makes about a twelve-hour workday.

I make about $91 a month on the Casper
papers, and on *USA Today* I clear $22 to $36.
At my Country Inn job, I get $5 an hour, and I
usually work about thirteen to sixteen hours a
week. Then at Safeway, I get $8.83 an hour,
and since the first of the year I'd say I've aver-
aged about twenty-six hours a week.

So that makes a yearly salary of about
$13,000—that's barely enough for a family in
Wyoming. We have a mobile home. It's too
small for us really, but then it's ours. I'm making payments on it. I'll have it paid off in one
year. I pay $216 a month plus the trailer space
which is $135, plus utilities.

Originally, you know, I'm not from Wyoming. I was born in Yakima, Washington, and
raised in Sacramento, California. I lived in

96

Oregon ten years and I've been here in Wyoming about six now.

I'm six nationalities. Heinz variety. I'm German, Irish, Scotch, Spanish *and* Mexican, and Aztec. 'Cause my dad's father came from Spain and my dad's mom is an Aztec Indian out of Mexico City.

In our family, there was four of us children, two boys and two girls. I was the oldest, so I always had a lot of responsibilities. When they did something wrong, I was punished for it.

But the bigger problem that I faced was a nationality one, my dad being dark and Latin and my mom white and of Anglo people. We just experienced things. Like when we went to Yakima to visit my mother's family. I was pushing my cousin in the stroller and she was very white with a red head and some ladies came out of a department store and called me a dirty Mexican and spit at me. And then when I went down to visit my dad's people, I was sort of shut out because I didn't speak the nationality.

We were raised on farms and we had chores to do, and on the weekends we cut wood and got nightcrawlers and helped my dad. Everything was kept immaculate. He had white glove inspections in the house and if things got broke, you would be punished. He had a big two-inch belt. I have a scar here to this day from the buckle.

He beat my mom, too. Just for stupid little things. Like when she was ten minutes late coming home from work. He was a very mean person. He was a very unhappy man himself, an unhappy child himself. I can see that now.

I finished high school. I wanted to be a policewoman, but I was too short. I'm five even. See, in our society when I graduated in 1961, we had a lot of discriminations because of your height and your weight. In fact, I just barely made it into the service. You had to be five even and weigh over 110.

I went into the navy. I was a secretary/receptionist. And the service did a lot for me. It really helped me learn how to talk to people

and to have self-confidence. See, my dad raised us the old Mexican way where the man's the boss, the women don't say nothing.

I was three years in the navy. I didn't go overseas but I got to go places in the United States I never had been before. So for me it was a lot. I was on my own and it was different. Very different.

I met my first husband when I was in the navy. He was Hispanic and in the marines. We both got discharged the same day. I would have spent more time there, but I found out I was gonna have a baby, and then you couldn't have babies in the service.

So we got married and moved to New Mexico where my husband's mama and daddy lived. But I picked the wrong one. My husband just didn't have no spine. When we had a problem, instead of talking it out with me, he went home to his mother.

Maybe I was too young, too, I don't know. I was nineteen, twenty, and I wasn't really happy to be having a baby.

After we got divorced, I suddenly had all this freedom. It was hard for me to adjust. I had been so much under the thumb before and there were all these things I had never done.

I got into drinking. And it totally messed up my life, I'd say from twenty-one on up until twenty-five. I wasn't happy married but I wasn't happy divorced and then I remarried again and then I had one affair and then I had my baby boy and then I ended up stuck in New Mexico and then I got back to California. Then I had another boy and I had to give him up for adoption 'cause at that time I was about ready to go to the nuthouse.

Finally, I moved up to Placerville, California, and that's how I met Jack. And I met him in a bar and he liked to drink, I liked to drink, and I guess we lived together for a year and then we got married.

We used to fight a lot. Really bad battles. We'd try to outthink each other and smash each other's cars and I'd catch him with the girls and try to shoot him with a gun or wait

up at night with a bow and arrow for him. Just crazy things.

Still, I stuck with him, married and stuck with him. I don't know why. Probably because I'm not perfect and he's not perfect. We lived a hard life for about five or six years there, and I'm very ashamed of how I treated my life and my kids during those years. I just really screwed up to tell you the truth.

Then one day I came home and we'd been out drinking and the kids were crying and the baby-sitter was asleep and I looked at myself and I looked around and seen what I was doing and I stopped. Just like that. I can't explain it. Maybe the Virgin Mary talked to me, I don't know.

I became like a workhorse. I made sure we had things, whether Jack made money or not. I'd always find work, even when I was pregnant. There's always work. Whether cleaning a barn out, cleaning bathrooms. Some piddling little job. I had a lot of pride. I might have screwed up but I still had a lot of pride. I'd

only go to the welfare when there was no other way to have medical treatment.

Jack kept on drinking. He's a very big man, and he can drink whiskey, wine for two, three days straight. He's tried to stop. He has. He used to go to the AA meeting. But when there's no work and it's wintertime and maybe I complain too much that he's sitting on his butt . . .

Jack's a half-breed, half Shoshone. He was raised in a very lonely life. His mother died when he was three years old, and after his dad died he was raised in foster homes. So he has a story too behind him.

After Placerville, we moved on to Oregon, God's country. We had a little farm up there, and we worked in the sawmills. We were doing really good. But then the work for Jack went down, and he came here. He talked me into coming too. Now I could kick myself in the bottom.

But see, back then, five years ago, the oil boom was on. The population of Douglas was up to ten thousand people. Oh, my God, it was

unbelievable. People were making money like crazy. They were paying, what, fourteen bucks an hour plus travel pay, good benefits, the whole works. So Jack got a job in the oil fields, on the pipeline. And then what happened? The oil boom went down, the pipeline closed up. Jack was one of the last to go.

He started to drink. He got disgusted with our society, our government, and himself. He blew paychecks and unemployment checks and lied to me about money. And it always ended up on the same old junk, you know, fightin', and fightin', and fightin'.

Finally, Jack got in real bad trouble and got put away. That was two years, six months ago. He got into a four-day drunk and then supposedly done this certain thing which I don't believe is true. They charged him with third-degree sexual assault. No physical evidence. The jury was out twelve hours, but they gave him four to five years. It hurt me terrible. Because I knew he didn't do this one. I know him. If anyone knows Jack, I do. But because he's had a bad record and he's been in prison before, they just socked it to him.

The prison's 152 miles from here. I have to drive down there and I have to be there by eight o'clock in the morning. It's hard to even get a day off because I have to pay people to do my paper routes and things. But it's important for me to keep the family functioning.

While Jack's been in prison, my boy's got in trouble three times and my daughter's got in a little trouble, too. My son's a good boy, an honest boy, but he had a problem with marijuana and he got arrested, and he got drunk one day and burglarized one of his friend's house. Stupid stuff. Then with Marcie, she fights in school. They had to put her on probation.

I've been on my own supporting the family for nearly three years now. Sometimes I get terribly depressed. I have considered taking my life. Because it comes to the point where it seems no matter what I did, everything was going wrong. I felt that nobody cared. One time, oh, I desperately needed someone to talk to. They have a crisis line here you can con-

tact, and I went down there and the first thing the lady did was hand me a paper to fill out what my income was, what my insurance would cover. Now, if you're in a mental state where you're about to commit suicide, do you think you're gonna have time to fill out papers? I crumpled them up and told the woman, "I'm here to get some help, not to fill out forms. Do you want me to go outside and run in front of a car or something?" She just sort of looked at me, you know, like what's wrong with her.

I only have one kid left at home now. Marcie, who's spirited like me. She's fourteen, smokes like a fiend. My oldest daughter's married and living in Oregon. And my boy—who's turned eighteen—he decided to get married this year.

So with my son gone and Jack still away, I get lonely sometimes. Especially on holidays. Christmastime especially. And it's not just physically being alone. It's mentally. You don't have no one to communicate with.

But I do have my jobs and my daughter and my dogs and cats. And Jack'll be up for parole soon. He goes up for parole the eleventh of September, next week.

If they don't let him out, I try to tell myself that I can make it through another winter here. But I don't know. Sometimes I feel I can't handle it no more. I just can't physically and mentally. Because there's just so much you can do and winters are so hard. It gets so cold.

HARLEM,
NEW YORK CITY

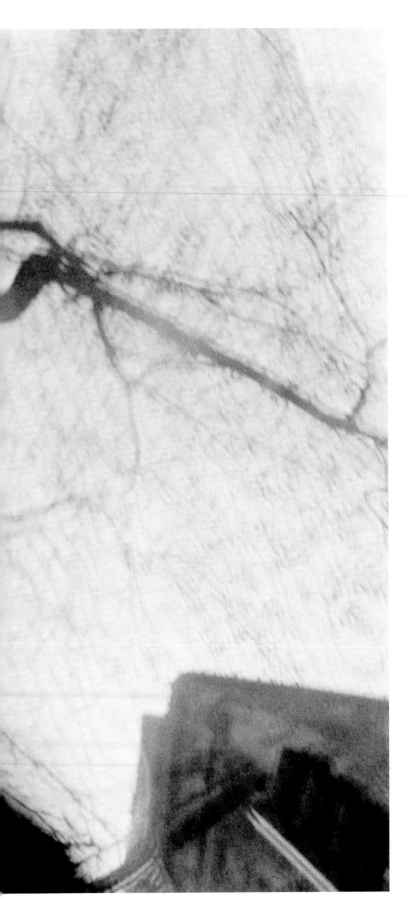

J. D. JOHNSON: I should have false teeth. It would really up my feeling about myself if I had false teeth, decent teeth. My teeth are in bad shape.

When you look good, you feel good. You look bad, there you go. Let's say you're out here, you ain't made a dime, the first thing goes, you hock your things. Then you sell your pawn tickets. Then you wind up selling this, selling that, just to make a rent payment. Then you're out of the house. When you're out of the house you're on the street, and when you're on the street you gotta get drunk or you gotta get high. You gotta get somewhere, because it's very hard to take. You have to do something. Just to get by the day. Just to get by the day.

A lot of things lead up to become homeless, see. That's what I want to try to tell you. Anybody can do it, anybody.

Like with me what happened was I flipped out because of my girlfriend, and then I blew all my money so I started living in my car. What happened was I got a good heart. It's a harder world than my heart, you know, and that's the way it is for most of the people who wind up homeless or who wind up on drugs or alcohol. It's because in reality they can't be that mean, to be mean enough to make it. To really make it, you gotta be mean.

But you see I did mess myself up too. Through drugs. I did a lot of different kind of drugs. From when I was a kid all the way on through. That's why I'm on a program now. Up here in Harlem. Some people say, "Oh,

youse was in Harlem," but Harlem is so beautiful in certain parts. I'm never afraid to walk down 125th Street. You oughta hear all the music they got playing, up and down, coming from the stores. They put their speakers out, it's a different world up here. I'm a musician, you know, and the only people really I relate to and get along with is other musicians or music lovers.

Sometimes I'll pull out my guitar and play in the streets or in the subway. One time I went down to the Wall Street area and had my coat lying down with a little bit of change. I was really wailing on the guitar and harmonica, and I drew a crowd and I got an applause and everything, but that's it. I didn't get no money. Just my change stayed in my coat. Super rich big timers! They knew what that jacket was there for. That's why I like Harlem. I go up to 125th Street and pull out the guitar and start singing the blues and I get money. They're great people up here.

I started using drugs when I was twelve years old and I was dealing at eighteen. I don't know why I started. Maybe it was just a reason for an escape from reality, I don't know. I was living at home, with my mother and father. They were hardly ever home—my father was a security guard and my mother was working too—and I did shoeshine in a barber shop, learning how to cut hair.

Right now I'm staying in Jersey in my parents' house again. For now. 'Til I get thrown out or who knows? And then I'll be back on the streets. Tomorrow you might see me in the subway. Or I might go to the park with my car. I was still living in my car 'til the other week by the way. I stayed there most of the winter. But you gotta be careful. You really can't trust too much in New York. People try to steal from you. They get crazy. Living on the streets can make you crazy. There's no doubt about it. It works on the mind.

That's why you cannot be homeless and live in a shelter. It'll drive you nuts. Like you heard about the Third Avenue shelter? All that's there is nuts and rip-offs, people that are waiting for that golden moment to steal. They steal your shoes, your jacket, anything.

I wanna stay in Jersey now for about a week, so I can eat a couple of good meals and sleep. But I ain't gonna stay. It's torture, too much aggravation. I get picked on and picked on.

See, my mother wishes I could be more like my sister. She's more successful, and I think they want me to be like her as far as getting married and having a stable job. But I don't want to be like my sister. She is more successful. But she's also more mean.

One time she took a label off a prescription I was taking and called the police, saying that she found drugs to get me put in jail, thinking that from jail I would go to the program. But I can handle jail, and I just stayed there 'til the next day when they called the doctor to find out that what I had was a legal prescription and that ended that. The idea was, that's how my brother-in-law cleaned up. He went to jail, scared the hell out of him and so he went into a program to avoid doing his time. And he's a great guy. I gotta admit that. My brother-in-law and my sister are very good to me but I gotta stop using drugs my own way.

I never stole from my family either, and my counselors even find that hard to believe 'cause there's very few drug addicts that will not steal from their families. I found other ways for making money.

I will not steal from my mother. She's a workaholic. Now she's working in a sweater factory making about $4.25 an hour, and they treat her like shit. She's fifty-seven, and about ninety-eight pounds. She gets sick but she won't go to a doctor. I try to get her to go to the doctor, but I can't. She don't listen to me. Like when I came back from Vegas I noticed my father used to go to the bathroom every twenty minutes. "Go see a doctor," I said. He wouldn't. I begged him, "Please go see a doctor." He wouldn't. Then I called up my sister, 'cause he'll listen to her. Finally she told him to go to the doctor. Turned out he had a cancerous tumor, and if he hadn't've gone, he would be dead today.

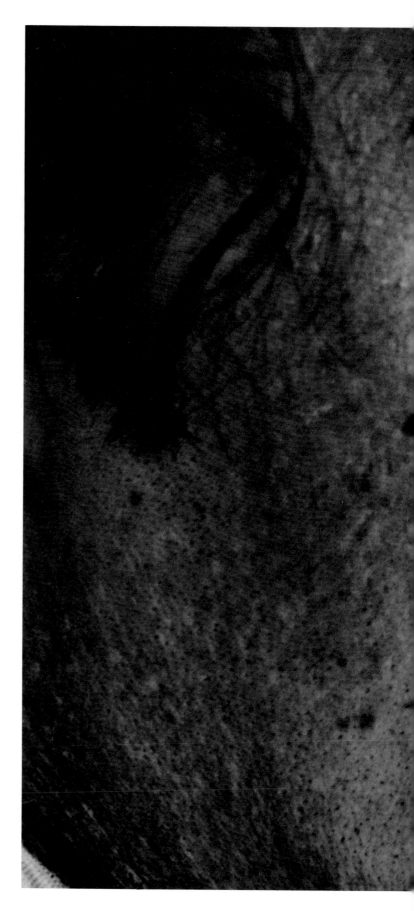

So do I get any credit for that? Not from my family. They still want me to be more like my sister. In my sense, I'm a better person than my sister. But as far as success . . .

I was not successful in school either. I was out working by the ninth grade. I had no-good teachers. They were crazy. They always said, "You're not going to make it." I don't know why they said that 'cause I'm a failure as far as grades, but I'm streetwise 100 percent, and I'm not unintelligent. I just don't care what happened in 1869. To me those things seem senseless, but evidently to the teacher they were important.

So I quit school. I was out working. I worked for a cable company and then for a dispatch company. And then I worked for—I don't know, I can't remember. Most of my life I drove a limo or a cab. Or a pickup truck.

But as far as things going bad for me, it was the breakup with my ex-old lady, you know, 'cause I really loved her, and then one month before we were supposed to get married, I found her cheating on me. I went through a total breakdown. I went and left Jersey. I shot a lot. I really wanted to kill myself.

I went to Florida, and California, and Las Vegas. I flipped out and that's what leaded me up to become homeless. I put myself away after that I think—I can't remember exactly. See, my memory's shot. I don't know if it's from having the breakdown or trying to kill myself, 'cause I tried a couple of ODs. I can't even kill myself. I tried three times and I failed every darn time.

I ain't got a girl now by the way. I can't afford a girl right now because of my position. I would not want a girl to be with somebody like me. Not a good girl. I downgrade myself. I meet mostly crazy type of girls, but good girls, I can't find them.

Sometimes it embarrasses me, being a drug addict. Some people are prejudiced against blacks, some blacks are prejudiced against whites, some whites are prejudiced against Italians, some Italians are prejudiced against

the Irish, but everybody's prejudiced against the junkie.

I'm not unintelligent though. As far as medical things go—as far as medical things go, I can save a life. If a person takes an overdose or something like that, I can save him. Like I put my neck out one time, saving this guy. First he took the convulsions, went down to the floor. The cocaine was fully injected into him. This guy he nearly died. I couldn't get his heart going. His lips were all blue, pale face, no pulse. But there was another guy there that had heroin, so I propped the first guy up, gave him a shot of heroin, and he came out of it. Now if he'd've died 'cause of that, I could have went to jail for murder.

It was no big deal to this guy though. I know 'cause I was in an overdose myself and you really don't realize the other person's saved your life. Like my friend George—he's dead now—he took me out of a real bad overdose—a forty-five minute one—and do you think I was grateful? I wasn't grateful. I was mad at him for throwing me in the shower and ruining my high. Can you dig that?

I ain't never been busted, knock on wood. I ain't never got bothered here. Not in Harlem. They're not going to put me down for having an itty-bitty pipe. They're looking for people with guns, they're looking for the big time. They don't want me. I don't beat on people. I don't hurt anybody unless they deserve it. What comes around goes around.

You know what some people call me? Dirty J.D. I'm not really a dirty person. They call me dirty because I have gotten over on a lot of people. But the people I have gotten over on are dealers, people that beat other people.

Sometimes a guy in Jersey'll ask me to pick him up a dime. So I'll go get it, but I'll only give him half and make five dollars. He don't know the difference.

I'm a con artist, see, but not like the rest of the world. They're all out there doing their shit on a much higher level.

Those people that come around at Christmastime and Thanksgiving? The Salvation

Army? Never give to the Salvation Army. I say that because I is poor and out of a home and I have to pay to stay at the Salvation Army. I have to pay for clothes at the Salvation Army that's been donated free.

I'm not doing my own cons now though. I'm on unemployment. I get $96 every two weeks, which is pretty good. I give my mother $20, $30, $10, whatever, and then it's $20 a month for the program. Then there's things I need for the car—insurance, tickets for getting over the bridge. You gotta use your money wisely.

My unemployment runs out in six, maybe eight weeks now, but I can handle it. If you're into the arts—just about every artist knows what it's like to be poor.

I'm an artist, I'm pretty good with the guitar, pretty good with the harmonica. Vocals —eh—not so good. I write music, too. Like I could sit here right now and make up a song about the water. First I'll start jamming, I might go into blues, I might go into country, I might go into rock and roll. Then I'll start going into how I'm feeling and I'll be looking at the water or looking at the horizon or what- ever is in focus and I'll pick up words. It might come out shitty and then again, it might come out dynamite . . .

Health-wise, I'm okay. I got an AIDS test done. I'm healthy. And when I told them what areas I hang around, it's the same areas that people have been that caught AIDS. I just hap- pen to be one lucky one. I haven't shot nothing in my arm for almost a year now. So I'm pretty good. Thank God. But if I had it, I'm not afraid of dying. To be honest with you, I know I'm going to heaven. I haven't done nobody wrong that ain't deserved it. I treat my friends right.

Some people say cleanliness is next to god- liness, but you gotta be talking about the soul, you can't be talking about the human flesh, 'cause a lot of people that are clean and mak- ing good money are killing people just to get in their position. Well, we're down here and we get a little dirty and scruffy, but the best peo- ple I know in the world happen to be dirty and scruffy and homeless.

HUGHES,
ARKANSAS

PORTA LEE DAVIS: When we first got to meeting, me and Mr. Will—I calls my husband Mr. Will—we was down in the woods. I was young, real young, about fifteen, and mostly he raised me. See, he was married when we met, but when he lost his other wife, he stumbled into me, and I don't know what. Finally me and him got married. I been married just the one time.

I'm the mother of thirteen, but I ain't got but five livin'. I had one or two miscarriages and then the rest of them was born into the world seven or eight month, but they only would live about a day or two days and then they would die. I asked the doctor why. He said I worked too hard and my body was too weak. He said they was short of growth or something. What I was, I passed on to them.

I was so hungry before I met Mr. Will. I was hungry so many times with my mama. She had so many children—we was eight—but she didn't have anything to feed us with.

So you know that big old flour barrel? I be so hungry, I take a spoon—there be no flour in the barrel—but I'd take a spoon and scrape the side of the wood and try to get something for a little gravy. And I was praying to Jesus, saying, "Please, Jesus, let me get a little food." Then I walked across the cotton field, and you know them plum tomatoes, them little wild plum tomatoes? I'd say, "Please, Lord, let me find one," and I take them few tomatoes and come on back to the house and I put them with that little flour dust—I knows there's splinters in it—but I was so hungry.

122

Sometimes I had no food for two, three weeks. A long time. My mama, she didn't understand how to vouch for us. She was a real church lady, but—she had a friend. He'd come to the house and be telling stories about how he was going to take care of us and all that and then the little money we made picking cotton, he'd get up and steal it. I was eight years old then. I was picking three hundred pound of cotton a day.

I was born in Blackton, Arkansas, not so far from here. I ain't got no schooling whatsoever. No sir, sure don't. My mama and brother and sisters all can read and write, but I can't. When I was thirty I went to school in Haines to try to learn. But whenever the old schoolteacher got around to me, I had a woman next to me read for me.

It was when I was only a child when I met Mr. Will, and he raised me on up. So I do all I can to try to see by him, and by the grace of Lord in Heaven, the longest I'm able enough, I'm going to see by him. I go fix him some food, put his clothes on, bathe him, and shave him. I cuts his hair, get him up, and walk him. I went to the place over yonder, the therapy place, and I see the way the rack is built for them to practice the walking. So I come on back and went out here and got me some sycamore posts and I dug four holes and put some rails up here for him to learn how to walk.

Every day I try to get him up there to walk. But mostly it be only a few steps, while the children be making a racket. They so bad. Then he wants back in the chair, back in the truck, or in the bed when the tiredness settle over him so, and he can hardly say a word.

Just this morning, early on, I carry Mr. Will to the doctor down in Forrest City. He worry me so. More and more he worry me. His heart be wearing out. He be bleeding all night long in the mouth and he be coughing a lot. So I'm sitting there with the childrens all day, 'til evening, but the doctor don't come back to the office. So when they closing up, they tell me to come back tomorrow. Like it no trouble at all for me to load up Mr. Will and the kids in the old truck.

They don't think I also have heart trouble. My heart was worrying me. I prayed and prayed, so when the doctors finally gave me the treatments, they found nothing. Still, I so tired.

I can't let up for a minute. This old house to put together. All the mouths to feed, with Cilla and Sandra being with us. They wild children. Aged three and five. Cilla with her runny nose be running 'round pulling up her dress like a little devil that she be. And keeping me in fits when I at work, afraid I drop a hammer or some tin from the roof down on her for she always underfoot. And Sandra so pretty but she a devil out there to drink the filthy water coming up from the ground and get dirty, no matter how much I put fresh clothes on her. You see those two don't look alike for sisters, do they? That's 'cause they got different daddies. Their mama, my daughter, lives over in the housing project in Hughes. Sometimes I go up to see her. She concerned that life out here too tough on me, with my man sick, but the rent there is too high and I don't like the city. There be too many people there, too much noise, too much trouble maybe.

Oh, if only I could find some place, some decent place. I get so tired, so awful tired, sometimes. I don't know what to do. I tried my best to fix this house up. I'm trying to make things better. Mr. Will will do better if it better here. I like cleanness and nice. But it's a whole lot of tough, hurting work. Hammering in the falling-out boards and cleaning up junk and ripping and putting down the roof. Windows be broke and leaking and needs to be put back in. The house once had four rooms, 'til the back just rotted away in the rain and wind. So I ain't got no place to cook no more. There a stove I moved in here by myself, but no gas connected. So I cooks across the street in the next house for now and carries the food to Mr. Will and the children.

We are here because there's nowhere else.

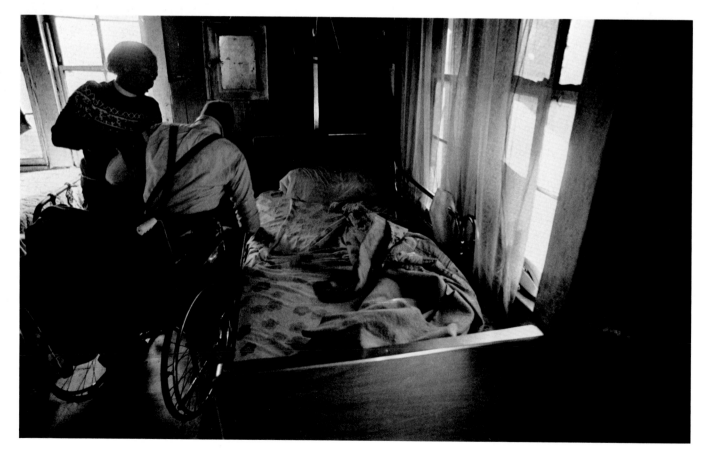

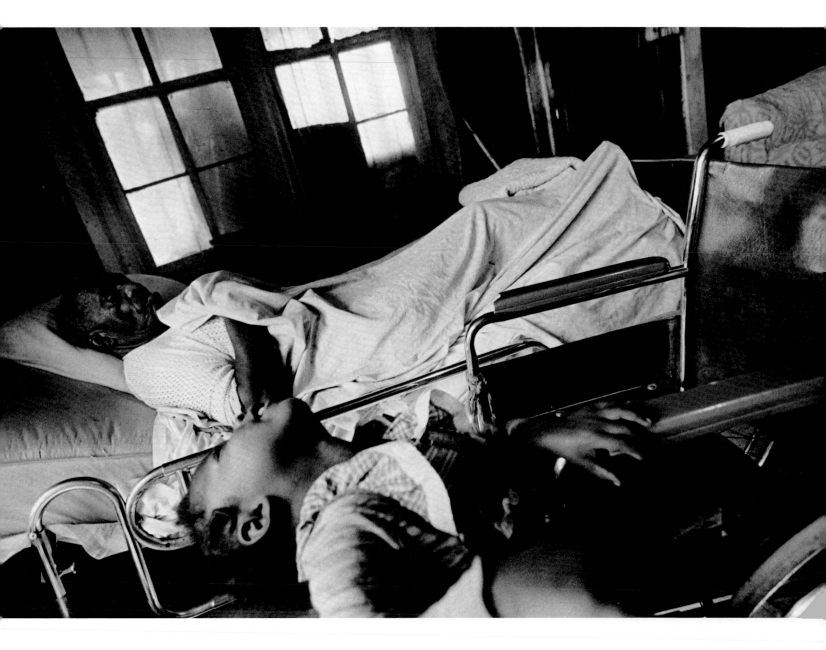

You look around here everywhere and you see houses burning. These farmers are making the people leave off the land. They make the tenants move, and then they burn the house down so they can't ever come back. I don't know really why they're doing that. I talked to a little lady up the road. She leaved last week. I said, "Why the man told you to move?" She said, "Well, he just wanted the house." Mr. Will says they use the house for kindling.

I'm getting on in years now myself. Sometimes I get so tired, I just sit up in the chair and sleeps. I be too tired even to get up and get into bed. I stay there all night long. And I pray and I talk to God and if I need something real bad I go get down on my knees and I tell the Lord the Creator who made me. And I believe that he hears me talk. Help might not be coming 'til the next week, 'til the next month or the next year, but it's coming. A letter might come in the mail and my children will be sending me a little money.

Or, maybe, say, like when we first moved on down here, about four years ago . . . We didn't have any food, but Mr. Will, he said, "Don't worry about it, just leave it to me and we'll get something to eat somehow." So he went to somebody's cornfield—that was before he got his stroke—and he pulled somebody's corn and we didn't have no grease, so he takes some hot water and puts it with the corn so it be kind of gummy and stick together. Then he got a piece of tin and he heat it and put the corn against it and make us some bread.

So if I don't have no money to get the little things I need, I don't let it bother me. I say the Lord given and the Lord taken and I say the Lord made everything, blessed be His name. That's what I thinks and so I wait.

WILL DAVIS: I be thirty-nine years old. That's right, sure is. Thirty-nine.

I was born in Mississippi. I don't know what town exactly. I lived around here most my life.

I been married about thirty, thirty-five years. I have much childrens. And all my life I been a working man. I farm. I was a great big farmer. I had about four hundred acres. Not by myself. There was other men.

It's been about, about five, six years ago I had my stroke. I imagine I had light ones since. I keep going back to the doctor. He checks up on me. I eats too much salt.

A stroke makes you real stiff. It draws your jaw, draws your mouth to the side and then you get so—well, it can kill you.

I been spitting up blood, too. But that little bit of blood, I believe, I really believe that little bit of blood I'm spitting up, coughing up, is from my bad teeth. From cleaning them out.

I like to sit out in the truck every day best of all. Keeps me away from the children. See my grandchildren they love me, they climb all up on me. I like to sit out there by myself and let the wind blow through on me. I rest there and I be thinking about my old life, past life, wishing I could get back to where I used to be, where I was years ago. I can remember things way back, back. Sometimes it make me feel bad when I get thinking about it. I wish I could get back—if I just could reach back down to forty and live from there on back up.

Back then—I liked to work for myself. I can't work no more and I don't like to go to the welfare and try to get a check. I don't like that sort of stuff. I like to get out and make my own money every day, every week, and spend my own money. If I wasn't sick, if I didn't have a stroke, I wouldn't be getting no welfare. I'd be out working, making a hundred dollars.

The welfare people, they treat you very well, but you still don't get that check but once a month. I get about $150. When I was a farmer, I was making pretty good money. I couldn't save none though—no, sir, you couldn't get that much. The big man wouldn't let you get that much. The big man kept most of the money. Always did. I'd be working sharecropper, something like that. Sharecropping don't make but very little.

Cotton crops, I picked. Me and my family

130

picked. Sometimes we picked three, four, five
bales a day. A bale weigh five hundred pounds.
A five-hundred-weight bale bring you about
$250, but you see, working on sharecropping,
you wouldn't get that on sharecropping. You
don't get no $250. You don't get no half of
that. You supposed to get half of that but you
don't. You raise the cotton and you picks the
cotton, but you don't get half.

You had to buy your supplies from the big
man, too. He had the old commissary store—
that's gone now—and he gave you an old re-
fund book, so you can go spend it in the commissary store. That book he gave you, you
couldn't spend it in town.

I got some children living around here. I got
children all over the country. I got some in
Chicago, some in St. Louis, some in Florida.
And I got one or two in California. My children don't help out much. They haven't got
nothing to help you with. By the time they get
through running around and taking care of
the wife and family they don't have nothing to
give. Oh, sometimes, they give a little dollar or
two.

Now my wife, she be hard at work taking
care of me. Some women don't take care. When
you get to be an old man, they're out looking
for somebody else.

She ain't my first wife—no, Lordy. I been
married many times before this. I've been married about four times. Some of them died. Most
of them just absolutely . . . I coasted away.
Because they was running around, spending
time with other folks.

My wife is young, fifty-eight. Some as
young as she is, why they forget about you.
But she stayed with me. Through thick and
thin, through sickness and death, poorness
and old. It's 'cause when I was doing good, I
done right by her. I give her all I make. So now
she don't wait 'til I get old and put me down.
See, I say I'm thirty-nine, but the truth is I'm
closer to eighty. And I think I'm doing extra
well for my age.

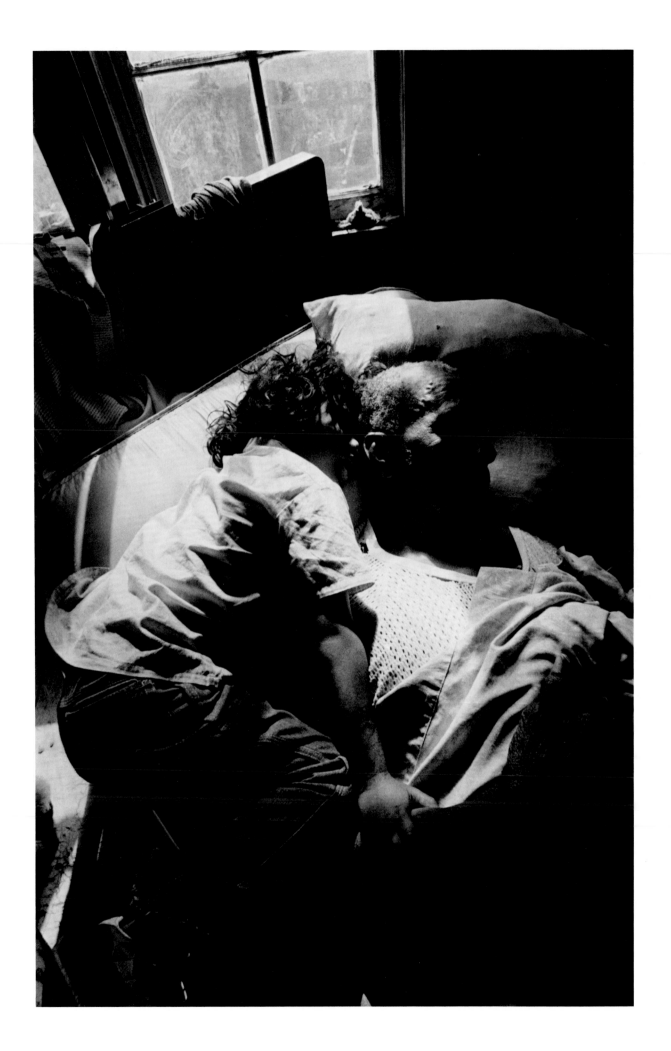

JULIA MARSHALL: I haven't got no life to tell.
All I know, I been down here working all my
days.

I been born here, in Lee County. My mother
had ten children. My father worked on a farm.
Sharecropping. We only had three boys so we
all was helping. I started picking when I was
five, but I didn't start chopping 'til I was nine.
Chopping's when you lay the weeds back so
the cotton can open.

I finished school through the eighth grade.
We went to the one-room schoolhouse. There
was about thirty-five or forty children, boys
and girls, and one teacher.

I been married to my husband—my second
husband—twenty-five years now. I'm fifty-five
years old. I had children with my first husband and then with my second and then some
in between. I had my first baby before I got
married. I was sixteen. I had eighteen children
all together, but I ain't raised but twelve. Four
of them died on me. Two of them died in miscarriage. I had eight kids when I moved down
on these hills and met my husband. He was a
woodcutter. He come down here helping me
cut the wood and then we just hooked up. He
says he been married before had seven kids of
his own but I didn't know his first wife.

Then me and him got seven children together. We got three, four dead. They lived a
little while. Well, one of them was born still-
dead, one lived three days, and this little girl—
she was born with seizures—she died at three
years. There's a cemetery back of a church
where we buried them.

My children started picking real young—eight years old—but they got more schooling than me. Now there's no cotton anymore out here and I got only one left home, my daughter Devon. She's seventeen and raring to get away. I think she's going to college when she graduates.

We're having a hard time now. My husband's very sick. He's had seven strokes, four heart attacks. The first in 1982 when he was driving a tractor for a living. Now he's almost blind. He can hardly see. He walks with a cane. I take him to the hospital for checkups. That's about twenty miles away.

We just get by on his checks. It's very hard since $347 is what he get and it ain't hardly nothing. We just pays our utilities and bills.

I can't do no work now. I needs to stay home and take care of him . . . Oh, I work in the garden, growing cabbage and squash and tomatoes and peas, black-eyed peas. But I don't like working in the garden now. The grass grow up and there's snakes. Big long ones—four feet. Blue rays, they calls them. I don't know if they're dangerous, but I don't like them.

I see my family sometimes. They come here, I don't go there. I got family in Detroit, all over. I got a son in the army. Six of my sons are living in Little Rock, but they've been laid off from the steel mill. My children doing little good for themselves. They now on food stamps and can't much help us.

I got thirty grandchildren and two more coming and one great-grandchildren. It's a pretty big family. I can't remember the babies' names. Some of them got them fancy names—Nicole and something else, I can't think . . .

I got a big family, but I'm not too friendly with my neighbors. When I drive by I waves, but they don't visit me, so I just keep on going. You gotta be friends to get friends and they don't want it.

Every Sunday I can I go to church. I dress all in white when I go to the church 'cause I'm an usher. My husband always come with me. He got his walking cane. He does all right. I

go at ten and stays until four-thirty. Sometimes when I'm on the program, I sings a solo. I been singing since I was fourteen.

We got fifty people in the church if they all comes. Usually we get about thirty-five. And we got a choir—twenty-three—mostly women. They take up a collection and a tithe at the church every week. To pay for the building and all. Some can't hardly pay the collection. We can't hardly pay sometimes. That money we gets—it ain't nothing.

Sometimes we travel to other churches. They're different but they're all Baptist. I drives in my car. We get other choirs at our church too. We have church dinners. Fried chicken, hamburger meat, pies and cakes. I don't have no recipes. I make it by heart. I throw in some things and I make it by taste.

I don't sew clothes. I don't know about them patterns—I can't make them right. I sews quilts, bedsheets, pillowsheets, like that. I make the quilt patterns up in my head. Diamonds, something like that. Like when I walk up and see a quilt, I can go home and make it myself. I just gotta see it, that's all. I sew by hand, and—after I got the piecework finished—it don't take me but about a day and a half.

My life's a little easier than my mother's was. We got running water for twelve years now, and I got a deepfreeze. Not too much has changed around here. A couple of people have died, that's all. A lot of people got sick—from heart attacks. It's from working themselves to death.

It gets very cold here in the wintertime, and we gotta find wood for the stove. My children helps me find the wood around here. I don't go out. The snow on them dirt roads—I can't walk on it, so I know I can't drive on it. That's why I put a lot of stuff in the deepfreeze—vegetables and all. And I buy a lot of flour to make bread. We can't go out. We can't even get to church. We just stays here.

I don't make no plans no more. He's very sick. We can't say, next week, next Sunday . . . All we can do is just pray.

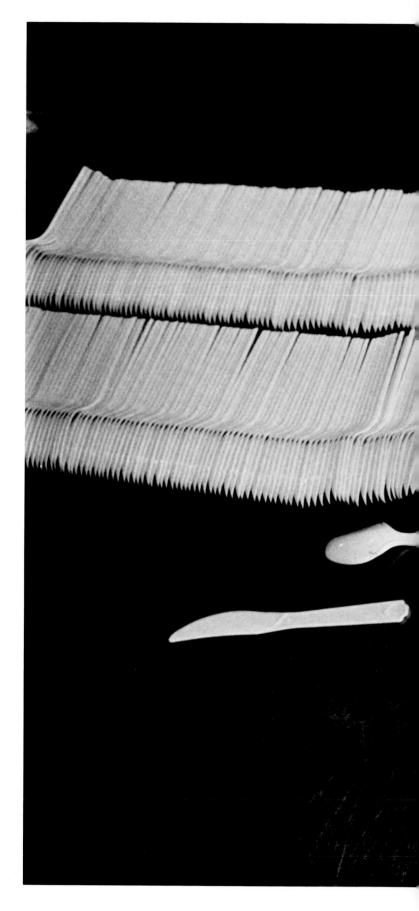

LONG ISLAND SHELTER,
BOSTON, MASSACHUSETTS

142

VINNIE BONO: I'm fifty-seven. I was born in the North End of Boston. I lost my parents when I was six.

I had an uncle. He was my father's brother and he was in love with my mother. She was in love with my father. In other words, there was a jealousy there.

So when I was six years old, I was in the hospital—I had scarlet fever—and that's when my uncle sneaked into the house. We had a cold-water flat then and he went up the fire escape, went in the house and shot my mother and father. He didn't catch my brother. My brother was asleep in the next room.

My uncle was arrested. He did life in the Charlestown State Prison. They put me and my brother in what today they call the House of Little Wanderers. I was raised there until I was seventeen. It was wonderful. It was run by the nuns in the Catholic diocese. They raised us up, boys and girls without families. We went to school, just like a regular, you know, just like having your own, living at home.

So I grew up. The only thing was, I seen people come and adopt from there. That hurt. I figured why not me? Is there something wrong with me? I grew up with that feeling. It took me thirty-odd years—'til I came here to the shelter—to find out that people did care.

I've been in this shelter since '81. I'm a night supervisor with the live-in staff. I make sixty dollars a week and my job is to make sure the people get showers and food and a bed to sleep in. I work from one to nine, five days a week.

When I was seventeen, I went in the service,

and that's how my drinking problem started. I went to boot camp in 1949. Like any GI, you get in with your buddies. They used to sneak me drinks 'cause I was underage. I used to go out and get pissed.

I was in the Green Berets. They had a demolition school, so I went to learn how to make bombs, blowing up bridges and all that.

We went to Korea. They taught us how to kill. They learned you one thing, it's him or you. So I kept that in mind. I made sure it was him. That's how I kept onto life.

Sometimes we'd blow something up, caves or something. Every time I'd be doing something, when them other guys all had canteens of water, I would make sure my canteen was full of booze. They never knew it. Half of us were all either junkies, on dope, or drunks.

Then one day I had a patrol. We had this guy from Tennessee on the rear point and as we're going by, we seen this North Korean girl doing something, probably taking a piss. The next thing, there was a yell and a shot and the Tennessee guy was dead. He had decided he wanted to rape the girl and she shot him. She was a North Korean soldier.

The North Koreans came and the next thing we knew, we were captured. They blindfolded us and put us on a truck. It was the most frightening day of my life. I thought I was gonna be dead right there. But they only took us prisoners and that's how I started my term in the prisoner-of-war camp.

In my compound, we were about fifty. Only thirty survived. They used to work us from sunrise to sundown. Digging ditches and working the wheel. They had the wheel to get water, and you had to go on it barefooted to run it. Many times your feet would come out bleeding. For food, they used to give us a bowl of rice and you had to take them maggots out. I got out on July 19, 1955. They called a truce. There was a bridge that connected the North and South. It's called the Bridge of No Return. We crossed that bridge when they exchanged prisoners.

There was this one captain who used to be in

the compound. He was no good. He had a bamboo rod and he used to always come in and whip our feet after working on that wheel. So I made a promise to myself, if I ever got a chance, I was gonna kill him. So when we were crossing over the bridge, there was this South Korean had a .45 automatic on his hip. So I stopped and took the .45, cocked it, and blew that North Korean's head off. I was crazy anyway. I didn't give a shit for life then. I figured nobody cared for me, or they wouldn't have let us stay in that camp that long. It wouldn't have taken six years.

After that, I was taken to a psycho ward. From there the Americans sent me to a hospital in Honolulu. I stayed there for six months and then they discharged me. It was an honorable discharge. Later they gave me, I think, the Congressional Medal of Honor.

We got our back pay. It was about fifteen thousand dollars, but I had no place to go. I stopped in a store and bought some civilian clothes and I went in a barroom and I started drinking. I was drinking, drinking, having a good time. I went to the airport. I asked a stewardess, where's that plane going? She says Aruba. I don't remember getting on the plane, but when I woke up I was in Aruba. I took a room. Then I found out there was gambling in Aruba, so I went to the casino and I lost all my money, all fifteen thousand dollars. It took me a couple days. I was drinking. I just didn't give a shit.

I got a job on a yacht on the galley, going back to Florida. When we got to Miami Beach, the captain paid me off, about $250. What the hell, first thing I did was go to the nearest bar. Three days later, I woke up on the streets, broke, sick. I was twenty-six. I started hitchhiking. That's how my life on the road started. I was twenty years on the road. Or thirty. I don't remember.

The first place I went was Abilene, Texas. Got a job picking fruit. Then drank and panhandled. Nickels and dimes. I went from Texas to New York and went down the Bowery. Seen all the people there sleeping on the streets.

On the streets, I had to learn one thing, survival. My teacher was old Foxy, from Boston. He learned me all the ways of the streets. He learned me how to do the telephone boxes; he learned me how to panhandle.

First thing you learn, you have to con your way. Like a street person, he'll never ask you for a dollar, he'll never ask you for fifty cents, he'll always ask for a quarter. 'Cause he's damn sure you have a quarter in your pocket. He's like a vulture waiting for the pickings. I know, I've been there. I think me and Foxy wrote the book on that.

I myself, I don't give no quarters to street people. They tell me they're hungry, that's a lot of crap. Don't believe it. A street person knows where to go, where there's churches and missions. I kept on traveling. I went to Trenton, I hitchhiked to Arizona. I had a woman now and again. Only when I was sober though. Then every time I would drink, I would get sick. I didn't know what was happening inside me. I

would throw it up and drink it down again. It was getting so there was no taste to it.

Then I seen this railroad, I seen guys getting on the boxcars, I said, why don't I try that? So I went down the embankment and I seen my first hobo jungle. They took me in, made me wash up. They showed me how to jump on the boxcars, how to get off. We used to go into town, look for work and panhandle. And when we made something, we'd bring it back. We'd share everything we made.

I was a hobo for ten years. Sometimes I stayed four or five days on a boxcar. You make your own ventilation. I always carried a knife and I used to make holes. But you couldn't cook, you'd burn the car up. You ate cold beans, things like that.

Then one February, I hitchhiked up to Boston. When I got here, I was hurting inside. It was eighteen above zero and I had only a short sleeve shirt on, Bermuda shorts, and sandals. Everybody was looking at me like I was crazy. Then a cruising car pulled up and

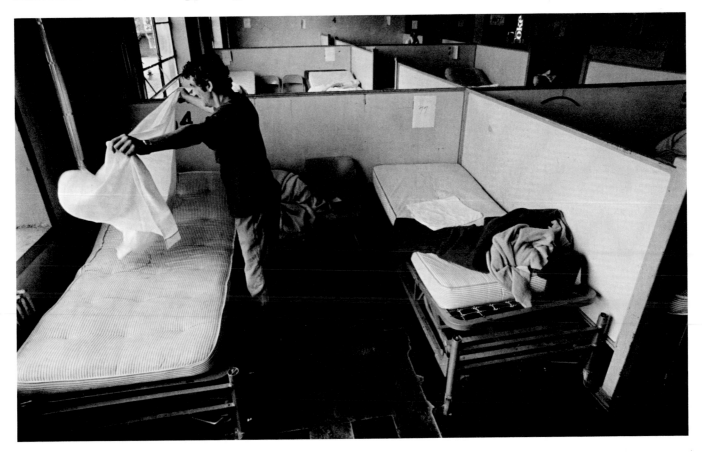

the police asked me what I was doing, dressed like that. I said, "Oh, I'm walking up to go to the hospital." And when I said that, I passed out.

When I woke up, I was in the hospital. I had been in a coma for fourteen days and they told me I was going through what they call the d.t.'s. I was hemorrhaging, I was passing blood. My liver was infected and everything.

After I was better, the doctor told me, "You've got no place, why don't you go to the shelter?" That's when I started a brand-new life, a new living. I went to the shelter at the Boston City Hospital. There was fifty, sixty people, all on one floor. The women would sleep on one side and the men would sleep on the other.

I used to go there at night, come out during the day. So one time I asked the director, I says, "Can I help out?" He says, yeah, okay, and he gave me a job, helping around the shelter, cleaning it up and everything. He saw I took an interest.

I wasn't drinking no more. 'Cause I had no money and I wanted to stop. What changed me was coming close to dying.

Then they moved the shelter out here, to Long Island Hospital, and the director told me, "I want you to go down and help clean the building and so forth." So I went and I been here ever since. We live in a dorm. I got nice clean clothes. I enjoy the work. It's a regular job and it ain't that hard. These people are my family. We're all from the same streets.

When I'm feeling depressed, angered, uptight, I go down to the statue. It's a statue of the Blessed Mother. I sit down there and just look at it, and after awhile, it makes me feel good. My depression goes away, my anger's gone.

I saw the Blessed Mother when I was going through the d.t.'s. She was a ray of hope to me and she said, "If I cure you, you have to do a favor for me which is to help other helpless people." I kept it in my mind all the time and I've been doing it ever since. The only way I'm gonna stop is if they close this place.

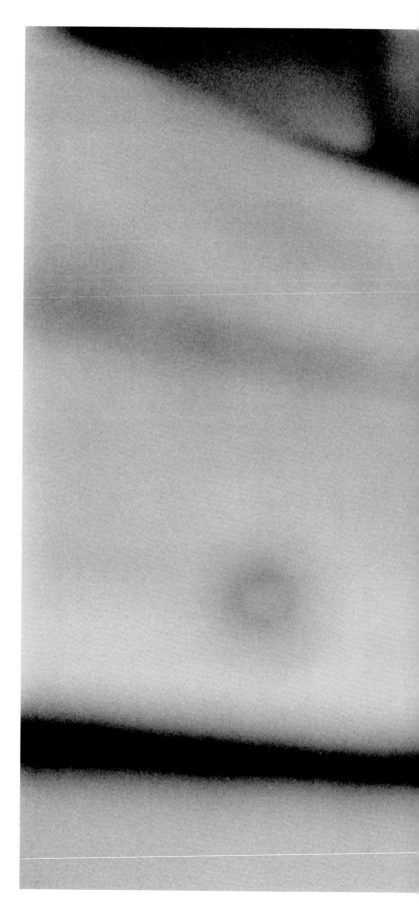

We get about 360 people at the shelter, men and women. We have 40 percent mentally impaired people and 50 percent alcoholics and 10 percent just people who think you owe them a living. 'Cause a lot of them just don't want to work. They want things but they don't want to pay for it. They can get forty-two dollars every two weeks from the welfare, even if they don't have an address. So that's enough for them to get their booze on, their dope, and they can come out to the shelter free every night. This is not the people in their forties and fifties, this is the guys in their twenties, early thirties. Those same guys are the ones that'll rob you.

It's not dangerous in the shelter, though. It's quiet, people scatter around, watch TV, play cards, and talk. It's like any place else though. They see something that's not nailed down, they're gonna lift it.

A couple of years ago, I met a woman at the shelter and we got married. Her name was Sharon. She was homeless, too. I just seen her, hey, she looked so nice, it was something I wanted. I figured it would make a nice something to get together and have a companionship.

We got married right here in the shelter. All the staff was here. Then we got ourselves a little apartment in Dorchester and we was going good for awhile. I wasn't drinking. I was clean. She was clean. We were both working here. We paid the rent, we bought the food, we had a bank account, about five hundred dollars.

Then one day I went home. I opened the door. Now, we had a radio with the speakers on it. I don't see that. So I looked around and I see her keys on the table. I said, oops, something happened.

What she did was took her paycheck and the five hundred dollars and left. See, a homeless person will never settle down.

She never came back. She just went. I felt hurt. I said, "Lord, what do I do?," and the good Lord says, "Don't touch the booze, just keep going forward . . ." So here I am back at the shelter.

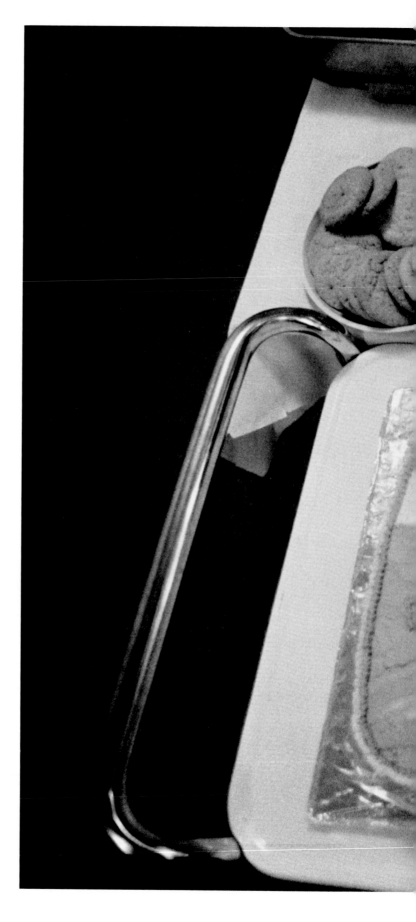

CREIGHTON,
SOUTH DAKOTA

ED EISENBRAUN: Around here, when someone's moving who's lived in this community for any length of time, it's customary to get together to bid farewell, wish them well. Everyone just gathers in a church or someone's living room to, I guess just to show that they care. We oftentimes think that people don't care when in reality they do. And we've just had so many friends come to say good-bye, and the number of calls and stuff we've received . . . Even on a night like tonight, with the snow running deep on the roads, so many friends are here at Emmanuel Lutheran to say good-bye.

I guess the thing that's really impressed on me the most are the number of people that have come up and said how much they admired us making the decision that we made. In the back of your mind, you know, there's always the worry of being rejected by your peers. You perceive they're thinking this or thinking that when in reality they're happy for you. I don't think there's ever been a rumor around our community that would indicate we just went broke. There's always the gossip, of course, but people have been overwhelmingly supportive. That's important to me. I'm very self-conscious, very proud, and I guess if you want to analyze me psychologically, I'm a person that does not like to be put down.

My family's been in these parts, farming and ranching, for three generations. Our particular community was homesteaded by my grandfather. He had five sons and most of those sons all resided in the same area and it

was a pretty close family. In fact, it was real close. We would love to stay and preserve the traditions that have gone on. But the cold hard facts is we can't. Not if we're going to survive.

I'm not that old, but as I grew up we had neither electricity nor running water or any of the modern conveniences that we all so enjoy today. One of my jobs was to go out to the old well and pump water. Well, we had a windmill, too, so when we had plenty of wind, the windmill did the pumping, but there were many times I'd have to pump with the handle.

My wife Linda and I grew up in relatively the same neighborhood, about fifteen miles apart. But her life was a little bit different from mine insofar as they were more isolated than we were. They lived in ranch country, real rugged, along the Cheyenne River. They only had one neighbor and that neighbor lived about three miles from them, and the next closest neighbor was about ten miles away. So in her childhood, outside of school, they just never seen any other people.

Linda comes from a large family. She had eight brothers and sisters, and being the oldest, she had to take on more responsibility than a kid normally would. As soon as she was able she learned to drive a tractor, to mow and rake hay, to ride horses, to cook.

About the time I was ten years old, I had quite a few companions up in our neighborhood. Through with our chores, we'd get on our horses and play our share of cowboys and Indians and make-believe stuff. Then every summer, in August, we used to get together and our parents allowed us to take a little camping trip. That was something I just lived for. Me and a few of the guys usually headed towards the river breaks or another isolated part of the country, and for three days we'd camp out. There isn't a square foot of country around here we haven't rode over.

After those formative years, of course a person has to start being more responsible and I had some good teachers. My father was a good teacher. He was a rancher, but also a busi-

nessman, having owned a little country store for a time. He not only taught me the art of ranching and farming, but also how to be a businessperson. While still in school I started buying some livestock, then after the National Guard I was out to try to build a future.

And after a fashion, Linda and I met. They finally cut the weeds down along the river and me and my family seen there was quite a family down there. And one girl particularly got my attention. And of course that was Linda. And after about three years of courtship, she and I were finally married.

In the first few years of our married life, we found out what life is really about. When you go into business, of course, you have to borrow, and we were indebted from almost day one. And then Mother Nature was not real kind to us. We were aware, living in an arid area, that you're going to have to fight the elements, but in those first five years hailstorms completely cleaned out our crops. It was devastating. It kind of shaped the rest of our lives.

It forced us to diversify into areas we hadn't planned on. We got into the dairy business. We had a growing family at that time. We had two kids and we needed some way to support ourselves. And we found that we had to depend more on each other and on our neighbors. Losing all that income, we couldn't buy the things that were necessary to run the farm, so we borrowed equipment and stuff and offered our labor in return. And we found that to be one of the best of all things, that in working with your neighbors, you get together, you have a little fellowship along with it.

You know, everything's seasonal. Starting in the spring, there's calving time and then about May the circuit of branding. Then you get your haying and your harvest seasons. In September, it's start seeding wheat or putting in your fall crops. And then along November, December the snow hits and it starts cattle feeding time. Of course I don't really care for snow and cold weather but it brings good get-togethers—and cribbage season.

If you've never played a game of cribbage, you've never really lived in the West. Cribbage season usually opens the middle of November. After dropping their kids at school, the neighbors would stop by at nine in the morning. They'd have their chores done and we'd sit down and sometimes play and tell stories 'til three in the afternoon. You just kind of lose yourself. That's the stress release I think of in rural America. We'd drink tons of coffee and eat lots of homemade soup. We'd just look for an excuse not to have to go outside in the cold and that seemed to be one of the better ones.

That kind of thing makes you realize just how valuable neighbors are. Living out here, despite the miles between us, you don't much feel the isolation. And that close association you develop . . . Well, you probably don't realize how close it is until you have to leave.

We've been eighteen years on this ranch, and you know our kids grew up under pretty much the same conditions that we did, outside it wasn't quite so primitive. I mean they never experienced life without a television or electricity or a telephone. But they all attended the same rural one-room schoolhouse that I attended, an experience that I've never regretted and I don't think they will either.

My kids started riding their horses as soon as they were big enough to walk. They did a great deal of that, although later, the mechanical horse—and I'm talking about the motorcycle—came in. See, as things modernized, so did we. But the same beauty of the country was still there. And on our particular ranch, one place that the kids and I used to like to go, just before sundown, was a ridge west of our home. We used to ride up there and look off at the Black Hills jutting out of the landscape. Oh, on a clear day . . . What a beautiful sight. Bear Butte would stand out all by itself, that lonely butte. What a sight.

So we had some good times, real good times. But in the area where we live, you can never count on anything. We're at the mercy of the weather. Weather is one of our biggest enemies. Either it was too dry, or—well, of course

I can't say it was ever too wet in this area—but there were a lot of times it was too wet in the spring and we couldn't get our hay out. We'd have the hay on the ground and then we'd get just enough moisture to eventually destroy the nutritional quality. But droughts have played more of a role in shaping our lives than any other thing, and we suffered through some of the worst times in recent history.

We were almost forced out of business a couple of times. Twelve, fifteen years ago, it was real serious. I got outside employment. First I sold retail food, livestock supplies, just out the door of the house and then I worked as a district sales manager for a livestock feed supply company.

I didn't run the farm then, Linda did. I was home on and off but she basically ran the entire operation for three years. Then it just wasn't working out and we were really torn. I wasn't making enough to justify leaving the ranch and yet the ranch wasn't making enough to support itself.

So that's when we went into the dairy business. We went through some really hard times initially. And then, finally, there were a couple of years, two years, that things went along pretty well, so we upgraded our facility, modernized, and we began to show a profit.

It didn't last though. Beginning in '80 we had some dry years, and then, along '82, we had the wettest year on record. Then in '83, we began a kind of landslide. The markets became very depressed—the livestock market dropped, the grain market dropped. Then '83, '84 were dry years. Roughage crops were very poor, particularly the hay, and with the business we're in, the dairy, it requires a lot of roughage and we had to buy most of it. And then in '85, we had an extremely dry year and on top of that, there were the grasshoppers. They did as much damage then as they did in the infamous thirties.

Grasshoppers will feed on anything green, tender. They'll start with the best and as that supply runs out, they'll eat just about anything. And I think a grasshopper will eat five times its own weight per day, so if you have them in large numbers, it doesn't take long.

Well, along in the spring of '85, it was a do-or-die situation. And we had decided in April that if we hadn't received moisture by June, we were actively going to look at another profession to get into. We sat the family down and discussed the situation and of course, the immediate reaction of our teenagers, well I should say they were all teenagers but one, was, "Oh, no way, we don't want to leave. There's no reason to leave." But the cold hard facts were we had to do something.

Well, as I said, you know it was a do-or-die situation. May went by, June went by, and as June passed it became evident that it was going to be an extreme year, and it ended up being one of the worst years that we had ever experienced in our eighteen years on the ranch, as far as drought. We didn't put up enough hay to feed our livestock and what little forage we had wasn't worth processing

into feed, so we just allowed the cattle to graze it. And by August I started seeking employment.

I guess one of our main criteria was we wanted to find something that would continue our family association. You know, a family-type business. And we decided we might like the motel business. So I interviewed a few places and in September I was notified that I had received a position at a motel in Bismarck, North Dakota.

It's been tough. All of it. The day I sold the last of my livestock was probably the saddest day of my life. I had a real closeness with our livestock, especially with our beef cows. We had put together a good set over the years, and it was something I took a great deal of pride in. I was able to stay composed and get the cattle loaded and the trucks rolled out and that was it. Finally, I had to let my emotions go. I isolated myself for a few hours and looked around and realized that reality had arrived.

I'm that kind of a person, you know. When things really get bad, I kind of isolate myself and think, cry, laugh, get mad, whatever it may take, and then I'm fine. I'm ready to go again. And I guess in a way, selling those cows was like burying a close member of the family. I don't like to compare animals and humans but this was something we had spent a life, a whole lifetime putting together and in a few short moments, it was all over with. We were in mourning, bereaved.

But we knew we had a job to do. We started packing. I'm not a person that's ever going to enjoy packing. We have too many possessions and we're two big pack rats. We're very sentimental. Every little item has its special meaning or thought and it's real difficult to dispose of anything. We packed up an awful lot of stuff we should have left behind.

Then came the big moment. Dad took down the family sign. We had to say good-bye to the place. The house, the buildings, the old pet dog, everything around us. I just kind of walked through. Walked through, and just plain cried.

It was the same for Linda. Maybe worse. Her roots are probably planted a little deeper than mine. I've always been a person that's enjoyed looking to see what's over the next hill while she's more a person who's liked to stay in one place.

The neighbors came to say good-bye. We had a horse trailer and a moving van and another small van and one neighbor's farm truck. We had quite a cavalcade of things going. And up to this point, the kids had never really accepted the fact that we were leaving. They didn't want to go. They resisted up to the last hour. We literally had to force them into the truck.

On the ranch, you know, you look around and the beauty is indescribable. It's everywhere, even in little things. But now, all of sudden, we're faced with the reality of having abandoned all that. All that beauty and all that freedom. There it goes, it's gone.

INGLEWOOD,
CALIFORNIA

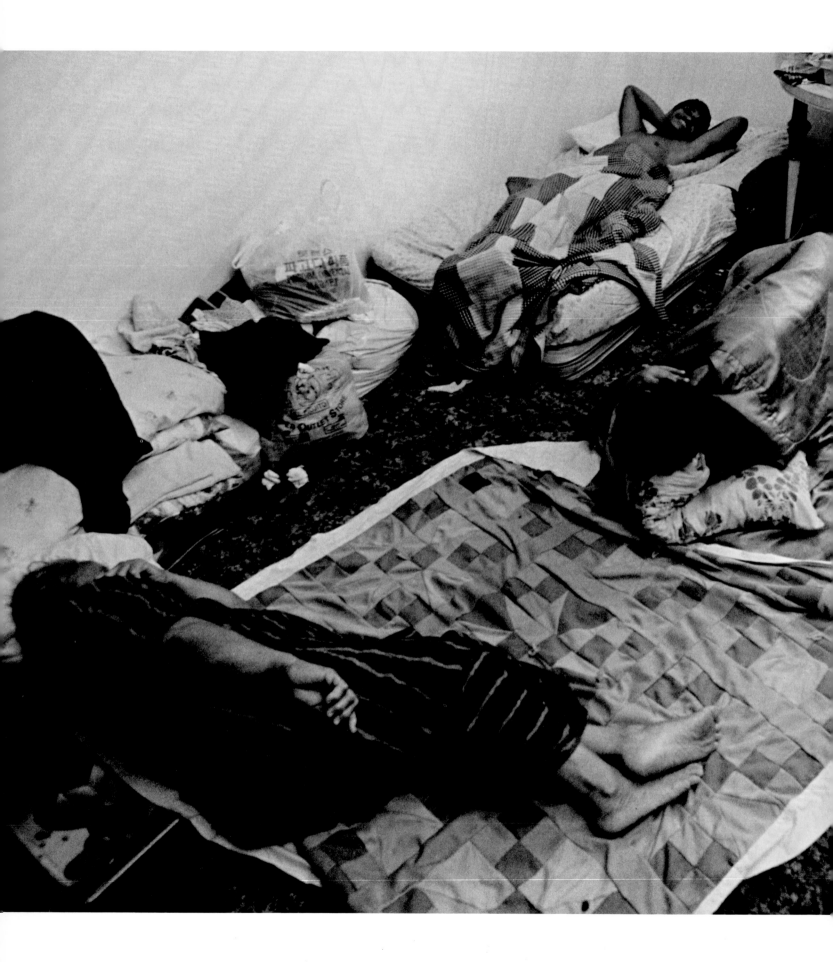

VEHIKITE TULIKIHIHIFO: Me and three kids and my mother sleep in this room. Each room has a family.

There are twenty-two people living in this house. Two people working: my brother Sateki and his wife. Sateki is number eight of the children but oldest man here. As oldest man, his duty is to collect the family together and keep them together. He works as a mechanic. His wife works, too. They work for the same company, but the wife, she's in the office, she works for the computer. They the only two working here. We depend on them. That's the Tongan custom.

Before I came from Tonga, I thought that America was the same as Tonga, because in Tonga, if you come over to stay from another place, you can eat and you can sleep. You have to bring nothing. And I expected America is like that. I expected I could get the food in easy ways and I expected I could get a car or something like that.

In the island, if you have a horse, and your neighbor comes over and asks you to give him the horse, you're gonna give him the horse. For nothing. And I expected America was the same. In the island, we can come over and stay for however long we can stay. We stay for nothing, we eat for nothing, we don't owe any money. That's the Tongan custom.

Tonga—that's the name of the island that Captain Cook discover in 1777. He name it Friendly Island, because the people is really friendly. When you meet them they smile all the time. They feel anxious to give all the time.

169

The island of Tonga before, it was a civilized island. Because when the white people came down there, we already had a good life. The white people, they say they brought the toothbrush. But in the island, we have a kind of tree that we use to make a toothbrush. Before the white people came, we use that and every day we have it fresh. Again, the white people, they say they came with the plate. But we use a kind of leaves. When we get ready to have our eat, we bring the leaves, and after, we throw them away. So everything was already in the island when the white people came down.

My husband's still in Tonga. He's not really in perfect health. He don't have any energy. His body's weak all the time and he's coughing a lot. My brother, he gives me money to send for my husband. So maybe later, he comes.

I came here alone with the kids, for them to be educated in America. Because in the island, there's a big difference. In the island, when we go to school, starting with elementary school, we pay almost everything. And when we get to the high school, the college, we pay more. Over here, it's easy to take the kids to school.

We have money in the island, but not much. Because now, in the island, the population, it's too much people. More, they grow more people, and the island don't have enough. Understand what it means. They don't have enough money.

When I first came over, I had no money, only to pay for the fare. My brother sent the money to pay the fare. But when I went to San Diego, I saw my brother's house, and I saw everything the relatives buy. And then I understand that in America, everything will be the money to get the gifts. And I know that it's different from the island. In the island, some people work and some people don't. But they all still keep the same life. But in America, it's have to work and get the money.

Right now, I still pay nothing, I eat for nothing, like in the island. It isn't hard to get work over here, but I'm not working because there's about ten little kids here. I ready them to take to school, prepare food for them.

The first custom we have in the island, the wife don't work. The wife just stays home, cooks, does laundry, cleans the home. The man has to go to the farm, to the plantation, work, plant, and do things there. But over here, the Tongan women, they all work because they understand if nobody works, they won't eat. And I expect to work here soon.

My mother's about seventy-six. She was afraid when she came here. She was really more than afraid, but now, she's happy, because almost all the children are around.

I have problems with my son. He's not clear in the head. The problem that happened for my son was when I was pregnant, there was high blood pressure. And I had it and the doctor, he take some blood from me and give me some medicine and I use it, swallow it, and I don't understand how long that I was pregnant. Finally, the baby came out the month or two before he supposed to be born and when he came out, he's like that—slow in the head.

Some kids in Tonga is the same like that.

Two or three, I think, not too many. Now, my son, he's a little bit better, because we take him to school in the island. Here, he's not in school yet because of the problems he had.

I like sewing, seamstress. It will be better over here than in the island, because I can work here like seamstress. That's how I can get the good life. I can make a dress to make money to look out for my kids.

One of my sisters is a citizen. A citizen can file the papers for us to get our green card. After five years, if nobody files the papers to get the green card, we'll have to go back, or maybe renew and have more chance to stay.

Over here, it's lonely but it's beautiful. Tonga is beautiful, but that's a little island. It's far more wide over here, and the chances are more wide, too.

But, it's hard to come over here, to speak English, to hear English. We afraid sometimes. But we like to be American citizens.

(Translated from the Tongan)

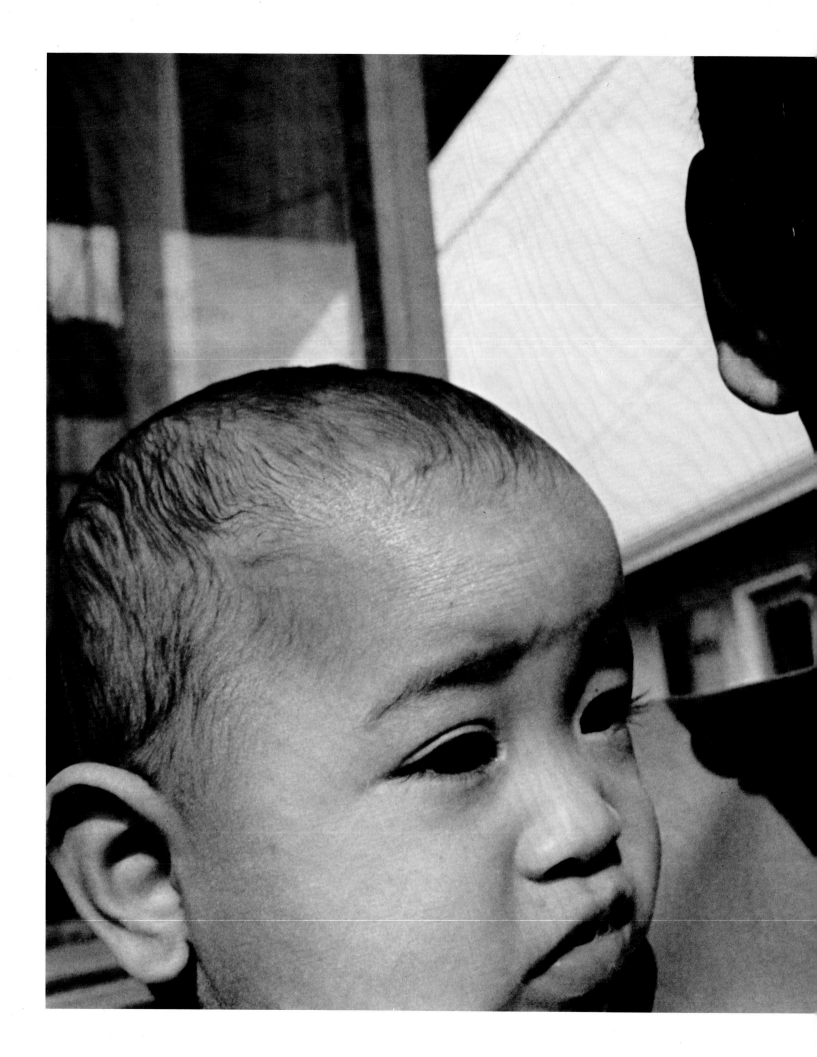

SHANTYTOWN, LOWER EAST SIDE, NEW YORK CITY

DELIA MILAGROS TORRES: Whenever I want to be alone, I hide. I hide in between the shacks or I hide in the trees and stuff, and I sit here by myself and nobody comes back here. What in life that's valuable doesn't hurt? Love hurts, children hurt. All those important things that are free hurt you the most.

Michael, my husband, can be a nasty son of a gun. I hate his guts sometimes. He can also be nice and sweet and lovable. I tell him, "I hate you, drop dead." Then I love him. It's very difficult to define him. 'Cause he's a wacko.

Michael lays a guilt trip on me all the time, all the time, all the time. He says if I leave him, he'll do something stupid, or he'll kill himself. And he is a nice person. With all the suffering that he's dealt with in his life . . . He's been through a lot of changes. He knows his mother don't want him; she dumped him in the hospital when he was a baby. She don't want him now either. And his father, he used to get drunk and beat on him.

We're not always quite the lovers Michael wants to make we are. He hits me sometimes, but that's all right, 'cause he gets his right back. I didn't use to hit him, but I've grown and I've got that self-esteem.

My full name is Delia Milagros Torres. Milagros means miracles. When my mother had me—her first child was stillborn and the second one was deformed and lasted only an hour—she promised God that if he would give her another child, she would name it Milagros. She prayed to the Virgin of the Miracles, and as such I was conceived.

I was a normal kid, seven pounds, don't know how many ounces, and I lived and here I am thirty-four years old. My mom was like any other Spanish mom, she got married to someone who dumped her. Her original husband dumped her, and then she had my wonderful father—beat and run, I called him—who dumped her. Then came my stepfather, the only father I knew for all my life. I loved the old man so much. He never hit me, and he told me I was his daughter.

I was raised on the Lower East Side, by Broome and Hester and Essex and Norfolk Streets, and we always had to work. My mother worked in the nighttime, she worked during the day. I've been doing housework and cleaning and baby-sitting since I was eight.

There was just two kids in the family, my brother and myself. My brother's gay. It's wonderful—he's Miss Victoria the Queen when he wants to be, and then he's Mr. Victor Otero, highfalutin, fancy dancing. Oh, he's doing very well. He never really had to work for

anything. He was maybe twenty before he got his first job. Because guys don't have to work in the Hispanic community, girls do that.

My father taught me to be nice and give and give and give and be patient and tolerant. My mother showed me violence. When I was little—you know those green cans with the soda crackers inside, mostly Spanish people buy them—she would take a nail and puncture holes on the outside and make it sharp like a grater. We used to have to kneel on that if we did something that she was not exactly kosher about. And then she'd give us a telephone book on each hand and we'd have to kneel straight.

One time we grabbed my mother from almost jumping off a four-story building. She barricaded herself in the bedroom but we managed to push the door open and we caught her one step out. I grabbed onto her leg and started pulling her back. We dragged her in and she started smacking us for it.

I wasn't my mother's favorite. From the time I was born she told me, "The only reason

you're alive is 'cause my friend was a thief and she stole the five hundred dollars with which I was gonna abort you." That's not exactly what every kid wants to hear. To top it off, I thought I was ugly. I was kind of coerced into believing that since I was a little girl. By my mother and my brother. One time my father said it and then he apologized. He said I was ugly 'cause I have crooked teeth. That always stays with you. What you feel as a child, you believe as an adult.

I didn't graduate from high school. Six months before graduation, I quit school because my mother was driving me crazy. But after having three kids, I went back in the evening and I got my equivalency and I got a year of college. I wanted to be a teacher. That's what I always wanted to be. I love children.

My first boy is not Michael's. I got married when I was eighteen to get the hell out of the house. And I wound up with some cruddy-duddy person that I had to support plus support a child. Then I had another boy.

I supported this man for a long time. Almost

seven years of that shit. I worked as a day-care teacher, and he used to steal my money, my money for Pampers and formula. He didn't want to work. He started using drugs, and I was supporting his habit and our boys. And I got my ass whooped lots of times. Finally it got to a point where I said screw this guy.

I left my husband. I left everything in the house and went back to my mother's. She reveled in my coming home. She rubbed salt into my wounds. She gave me migraines, I started getting an ulcer. I stayed in her house for a year and a half.

Then came Michael, Mr. Macho Man—Buttonhead, I call him, because of that hat he always wears, full of buttons. Good body, good looking, big head of black hair. And mean. And it's been a lifetime of knowing him, of seeing and dating other people, and rushing into dead ends. I've never been blessed with a lot of luck.

With my first daughter, I was molested. I had her with a man I didn't hardly know. She

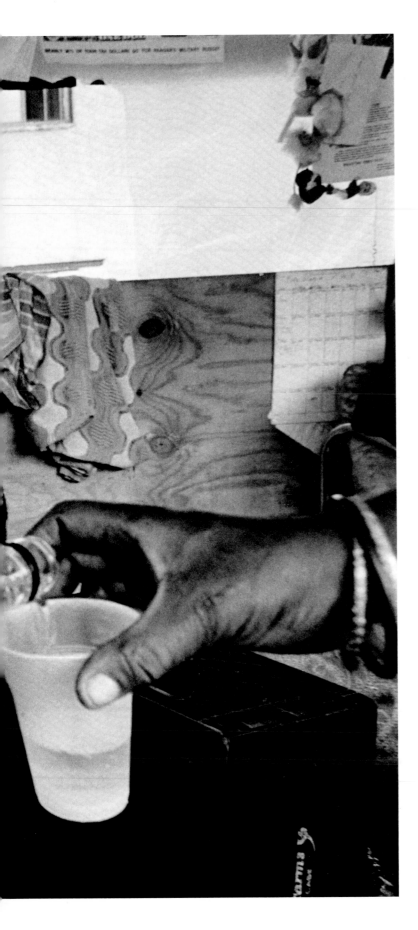

has no father's name on her birth certificate. But I don't believe in abortion. My second daughter was a mistake, too. She wasn't planned 'cause I was single, but I met somebody that I liked and I wound up with another child. That's Christine, that's Tutti. Michael helped me raise her as a baby.

Sarah, that's the real baby. She's Michael's. She is Michael. When she wants to be mean—boy, you ever seen a mean kid in your life? But she's gentle, too.

When me and Michael and the kids were all living on Tenth Street, it wasn't the easiest. But we never went hungry. Michael's a good provider. Then I lost my job through city cutbacks—I was an assistant teacher. Michael had already lost his job. He was collecting unemployment. Seven people living on $125 a week . . . We lost the apartment.

Michael and I started to rip people off. Not by hurting them, but by taking their money and giving them back something they didn't want. Scams basically. Nothing violent with knives or anything. Sometimes we'd do it together, like Bonnie and Clyde, but Michael couldn't get away with hurting somebody 'cause I didn't have the stomach for it.

I was always terrified on the street. I'm a scaredy-cat per se, but I got myself involved in it 'cause I was fed up. I was tired of being nice, I was tired of being sweet. I was tired of working and getting shit in return.

We got hurt ourselves a few times, don't think we just got away with it. One time I got really scared 'cause they almost shot my brains out. But they got busted, the cops came. Believe me, we quit shortly after that.

After all this, my mother was getting fed up and she went and informed the Bureau of Child Welfare that I wasn't taking care of my kids, that I was beating them up. They couldn't find bruises or anything, but they said I was being negligent. The kids went to live with my mother.

They were taken away three years ago. If I had them now, I would never expose them to a life like this. It's rough living here.

See, I'm getting immune to the heat. It's supposed to be ninety-some degrees today. But it's the cold here in Shantytown that's real, real bad. I mean, you're talking about iceberg, you're talking about actually not feeling your legs. Doc, the guy who started this place, got frostbite. He almost lost his toes.

In the coldest part of the winter, all kinds of people, homeless people, crowd in here to get off the streets. In summer, they can lay down anywhere. But when it gets down to zero and below, everyone knows they can come in here. The shacks don't have any heat, so we crowd together in the family house. We're all over each other, sleeping on top of each other to keep warm.

This can get hard on me. I get a lot of hassle from some of the men. They want to push that macho attitude on me, and they can't. That's one of the lessons that they learn here. That women have minds of their own and they're creative. They can build, they can do a lot of things. That's hard for them to accept.

One thing Michael has helped me discover is that I have a lot of strengths in me that I didn't know I had because I was always such a shy, stupid, wallflower paper doll. I didn't have no confidence, or self-assurance, or self-esteem. But I guess when you're basically the only female and you live with seven, eight, nine men, you have to grow up and stop being a fuddy-duddy and always sweet and good.

Michael realizes that I lost my babies because of my life-style with him. He feels bad about it, but it wasn't only his fault, it was my fault too. I miss graduations and first teeth and first steps, all those beautiful things, and it hurts 'cause I'm a fuckup. And I did it as an old lady, not as a young person.

My mother tries to turn the kids against me. She says I don't love them. She tries to buy them. She buys them dolls and she buys them clothes. So to them, my mother is this great generous lady and they won't even talk to me. That's why now I think I'm trying to be everybody's mother here in Shantytown. I have this mom complex.

The other day I saw my daughter Chris walking down the street with my mother. I was gonna call, but then I figured what the hell, if I call and she stops, my mother's gonna go home and smack her or yell at her or something. That's not worth it, that's being selfish on my part. So I just came home and I cried and bawled and bawled and bawled. I told everybody, "Don't talk to me."

MICHAEL CRUZADO: Basically Shantytown is a pit stop. You come here because you need a place to rest, a place to sleep. We don't charge you no rent. If you're not working, you have a job in the yard. Clean up, wash dishes, go get water. It varies how long people stay. I've had individuals stay here for about a week. I've had individuals like Joe and Sabu that haven't left yet.

The most that's lived here at one time is twenty-two people, but usually it's five. And it

has dwindled down to three—me and my wife and Sabu. Sabu, he's the guy with the broken teeth and the rosary beads around his neck. He works for a building super. He goes, he sweeps and mops the stairs, six floors from top to bottom. He gets a couple of dollars. He brings it in here. He can go sleep in his sister's house, but he prefers sleeping with us. Not because he likes living like this, but because nobody tells him what to do or how to do it.

Shantytown was started by Frank-O and Doc. Frank-O left the city. Doc still lives here. He's a chronic alcoholic. And I'll be honest with you, we are all alcoholics here. But we are not winos. A wino just sits on his ass and drinks. We all work.

What happened was, one day me and my wife were walking down the street. We were homeless. Doc spotted us and he said, "Look man, you can become my next-door neighbors if you don't mind living like this." He says, "All you gotta do is build your own little shack."

I looked at my wife and I said to myself, shit,

what the hell. At the time, we were sleeping on rooftops, parks, wherever the night caught us. They had taken the kids away from us. So it started like that. We've been here over three years now.

My wife became president of Shantytown because she is the most educated. Me, I never finished high school. I'm in the background wearing my button hat. You can say I'm like second in command.

We get men here 99 percent of the time. They come in and I tell them, "Number one, you watch your mouth; number two, that lady is the president; number three, she's *my* wife. This is not a commune, we do not share sex. You can't fight in the yard. You can call someone an asshole, but you don't pick up your hands and you don't hit." If someone fucks up, they wear the fuckup hat.

The police don't bother us here. They gave us a hard time at first, but then somebody from way up there told them, don't touch them. We've been in the media a lot. You know,

homeless people. Still, we have constant trouble. Young kids, their parents actually tell them, "When you're walking down there, hit them with a rock." Last week, they robbed eighty dollars worth of food while we were sleeping. You know how long it takes us to earn eighty dollars?

I used to go on the street and beg. I don't no more, for the simple fact that I have found other means. I am for sale twenty-four hours a day. Not sexually, but labor-wise.

Every day at exactly 6:18, I open the liquor store. The lady comes out of the taxi at Avenue D. Her name is Adele. So I walk her and I open the liquor store. Then I go around the corner. I help the guy with the coffee shop. I get his newspapers out and I open up his gates and he gives me a coffee for the lady in the liquor store which I don't have to pay for. So I give her the coffee and she gives me a dollar, plus a fifth of wine. So right away, if you're going to look at it value-wise, I already made $3.35 in a matter of fifteen minutes.

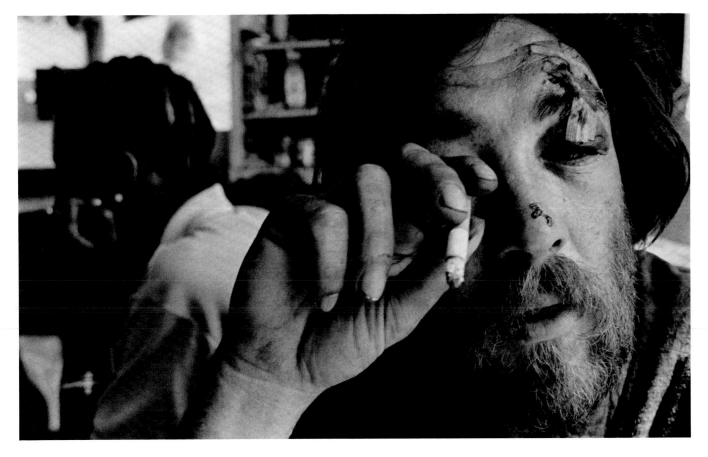

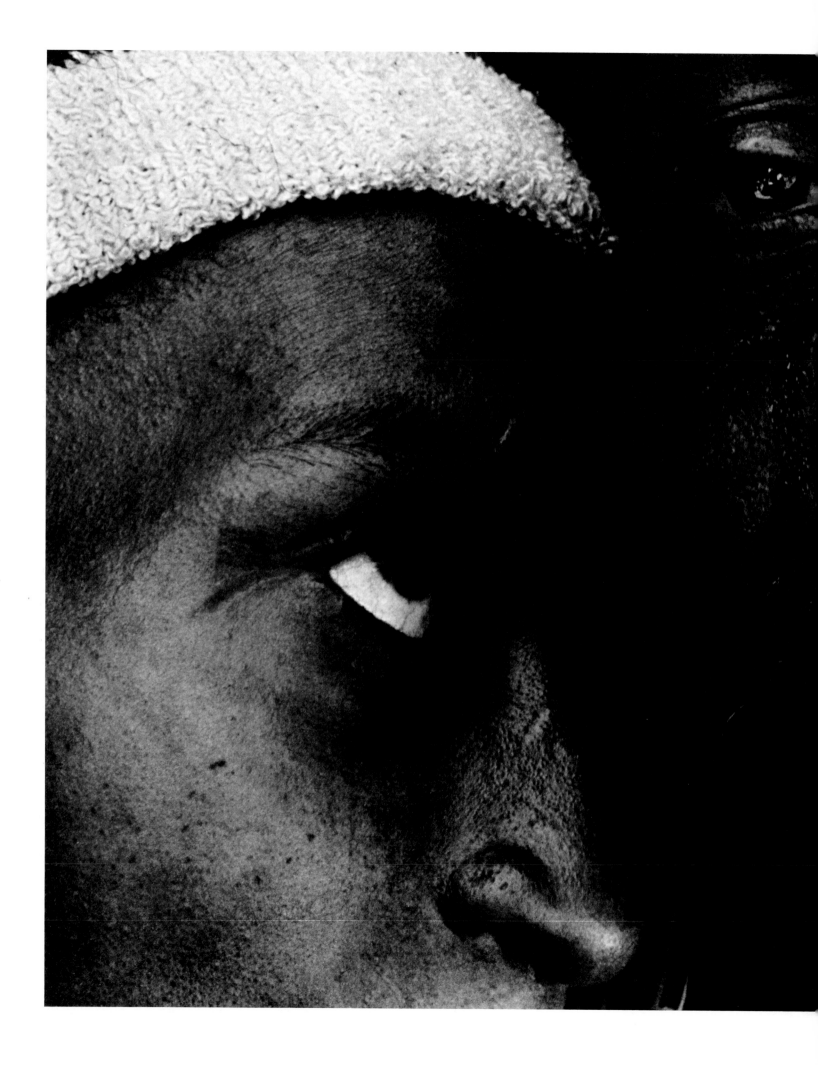

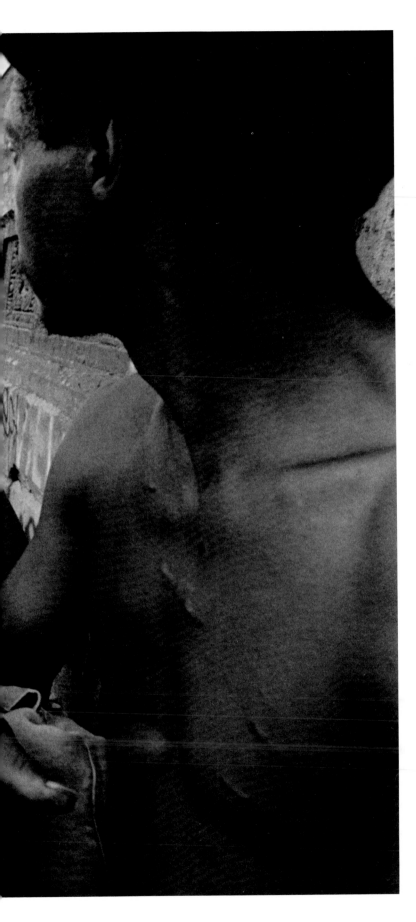

One day every week, I work on the milk truck. I start at three in the morning, finish at nine, and I make a measly thirty dollars, just enough to survive. Enough for food, wine, cigarettes. But not enough to afford an apartment. How can you hold a regular job when you can't take a bath?

I grew up around here, on the Lower East Side. My childhood was a bad one. My father used to get drunk and beat on me and my mother. He always thought I was a chump. He actually thought I was a sissy. I'm serious. My father was very, very tough. I have his anger.

When I was twenty-one years old, I broke my father's legs. I was walking with my wife and my first son, and my father hit me in the face with a set of keys. When I touched my face, I had blood on it. So I broke his legs, both of them, with my hands.

I've always been in trouble. Always. I used to steal from my parents. I would go into my mother's pocketbook and take ten, twenty dollars. I was a young kid. I didn't know.

I was sixteen when I left home. I went cross-country. My parents thought I was dead. They didn't hear from me 'til three years later. I did a lot of weird shit just to survive. I used to go to gay people's houses, play with them, let them go to sleep and disappear with whatever they had.

My first wife was eleven years older than me. We have a son; Glen, he's twelve. Then I met D again, and we've been hanging in there for a long time. I knew D from when we was growing up. I used to rob her brother, every time he came to the laundromat. Saturday mornings I'd beat him up, take his money, then I'd go to the movies and buy pizza.

I worked in construction for nine years. Then, four years ago, I got laid off—the same day when my wife gave birth. I got unemployment for six months and then I couldn't find work and the bills started adding up, and with all this other bullshit, I got so low down, I started taking drugs. And after eight months, I said, "Man, I don't want it." But in that eight months, I had lost everything. I lost my apart-

194

ment, I lost my kids, I lost all my tools, I lost my car, I lost my van. In eight months.

One day—this is how I got in the worst trouble—my baby was crying. We didn't have no money, no food, so I went to the grocery store. I told the owner—he knew that I had boughten there before—I told the owner, I was crying, I told him, "Please can you do me a favor, give me a dozen eggs, a loaf of bread, a gallon of milk, and I'll pay you back in the morning." He told me no. So I went back home and I took out my gun and I went back. I said, "Now give it to me." Then I went back home. Within fifteen minutes they locked me up, but I didn't care. I did it for my kids.

The wines have fucked me up. They have. I've been a heavy drinker for about a year. I need a quart just to get straight. Goddamn it, you'd go crazy in this yard trying to be sober.

Delia started drinking because I drank, and the wine's also hurting her health. She hasn't noticed it yet and I haven't told her but it has changed her. She's totally different than when I first met her. It's my fault. She never drank. She wouldn't even drink beer.

Her attitude is more bold now. She doesn't give a fuck. If you harass her, she'll smack you. At one time she would shy away, but no more. She's as delicate as a rose, but watch out for the stem 'cause it has thorns.

There's times when I have hit D. 'Cause my anger overtakes my heart. Sometimes I have to put her to sleep for a little bit. What I do is I put her throat right here, and I put this hand here and the other hand behind her neck. Basically I'm stopping the air circulating to the brain. It's martial arts. I done that to her about four times.

There's not too many women like my wife. There's times we get into a heavy fight, but I respect her and she respects me because we both know what we can do and we can do it better together than separately. If me and D was to separate, the struggle to keep Shantytown would be lost. She's a beautiful person. I love her, I adore her. I will die for my wife, for my wife I will die.

BROWNSVILLE,
TEXAS

GEORGE BORREGO: My store is like my fourth child. I opened it in July of '74. My wife, Vickie, was pregnant with my oldest then, which made me think about it a little. To open a new business with all those family responsibilities? It was frightening. But that was my dream.

I had started working in a men's clothing store when I was twelve years old, in sixth grade, and I worked through high school and college. Then I taught school for two years, but I made very little money, and I was getting ulcers from all the problems with the kids. So I decided teaching school was not my bag.

I borrowed ten thousand dollars from relatives, opened the store and did well. We made a profit the first six months. Then we went through quite a few catastrophes. There was a fire one Christmas which damaged about thirty thousand dollars of my merchandise, and there was a pipe that burst and wet all my stockroom.

Still, we prospered. In a year, we did over a half a million dollars worth of business.

But then, in '81, the devaluation of the Mexican peso hit, and my sales went from about forty thousand dollars a month to about five to six thousand dollars a month. That was devastating.

During good times, you see, about 60 percent of my customers are Mexican. We don't cater to them, they just come over. A U.S. resident might buy a pair of socks a month, but the Mexicans come over every six months and buy—used to buy—a dozen pairs, to catch up

for the whole year. They actually save their money to buy over here. Because the quality in Mexico is pitiful. The merchandise is just terrible, *and* it's expensive. So when they come over here, they're hungry. Hungry for clothes, for good lodging, for good food. They go bananas with McDonald's. The kids are just dying to have a hamburger from here.

The main reason for the devaluation is that Mexico started to depend too much on oil income. In addition, half of the oil income went into personal pockets. The last president of Mexico, it was calculated that he would have to spend over fifty thousand dollars a day just to use up the interest accrued on what he stole.

When I opened the store in 1974, 1,000 pesos represented $80. Presently, 1,000 pesos is about $2.10. That hurts. The middle class in Mexico is wiped out. A guy that is a manager in a bank in Mexico, he makes 100,000 pesos a month. Nowadays that amounts to $200, and after paying for rent and food, there's not too much left for shopping.

After the major devaluation in '81, we had other devaluations. Business just got terrible and it never leveled off. But we'd had a lot of ups and downs before '81, and those we survived. So not knowing that it was going to be as bad as it was, I made a decision to stay in business. I made a commitment that I was either going to make a go of it, or go broke. And I went broke.

Things just stayed bad and went worse. The U.S. government took three years to approve an emergency program for this area along the border and then after they approved it, they stopped making any other loans. They've only made three loans out of about seventy people that have applied in the city of Brownsville.

This situation is made even worse by the fact that there's a lot of bias at the banks. They won't admit it, but there's a lot of discrimination when it comes to getting the funding to operate. In this area, Mexican-Americans predominate in terms of population but not in terms of controlling wealth.

I now have no choice but to close the store. It's very scary. You get used to a certain lifestyle. Your kids are accustomed to certain things. Your wife is accustomed to being able to use the charge card. It hurts. We've had to cut down quite a bit.

We're not the only ones of course. We've had quite a few businesses close down—over two hundred I'd say. About the only ones that are doing well are the used clothes stores.

One of those guys has become a multi-millionaire. He buys clothing by the bales from the Salvation Army, rummage sales, churches, whatever, and then sells it for nickels and dimes and quarters. You'll throw your stuff in there and think that some poor people are gonna get it free. They don't get it free, they pay for it.

His overhead is practically nothing. He pays nothing in utilities—those places aren't air-conditioned—and he just dumps the clothes on tables or on the floor. It does though, in a way, provide a service for the very, very poor Mexican people. Eighty percent of the Mexican people are very poor. Nowadays.

The next three, four years are going to be rough for me. I'm going into insurance. The insurance industry can be profitable, but it'll take time to get established.

It's gonna feel weird not to go to the store. For example, I had to go to an insurance conference in Houston a couple of weeks ago and I don't have any navy blue sport coats in the store that fit me. So I actually shopped for a coat. I've never had to shop for clothes since I was twelve years old. But I actually had to quit shopping because I felt so uncomfortable.

So, the bottom line is, we're closing. But I'm not reneging on my debts. I've told my suppliers that after I take care of my family, if there's something left, it'll go to them. And no matter what happens, I'm staying in Brownsville. It's my city. I was born here. I was raised here, and I plan to die here. I already have my cemetery plots.

DOLORES GARCIA: My children. Ignacio's the oldest, he's fourteen. Esmeralda will be thirteen. Dolores is ten, Antonio is seven, Rosie, *la chiquita*, is five, and Jaime, five months.

Ignacio is very proud. He doesn't want to be called poor. He says he wants to go to school, to find a good job, so we don't lack for anything. He wants—how do you say?—to be an architect. I don't know why. Maybe because I have a brother who makes houses.

I like to be called Lola. And my husband, his name is Ignacio. We had never been separated. Not by choice, not by a fight. He was a quiet man. We never went out in the street or to the movies. He liked to stay in the house, watch football. No beer. Or we'd go to his mother's, then come back.

My children, my husband are Americans. I am an American. I was born in Los Fresnos, Texas. It's outside Brownsville. There were eleven children in my family. Three of us were born here in Texas.

My father worked in Los Fresnos and in San Benito also, irrigating orchards of orange trees and grapefruit trees. But we couldn't stay here more than ten days after I was born. The immigration notified us. My parents were illegal, so they had to go. But they waited, waited so they could baptize me in America. Then they took me back to Mexico with them.

I was fourteen when I came back here. My parents took all of us, the three children that were born in America, to show us our birth country. I went to live with my aunt in Raymondville, Texas, and my parents went back to Mexico. I went to work in the fields, picking cotton and all kinds of vegetables, and then packing them. Then I sent contributions home to help pay for the land my father bought.

I didn't go to school. In Mexico, I went to school for no more than four years. I was twelve when I stopped. But here, I didn't go. One time there came a man, he was like an investigator, and he asked me if I wanted to go to school. But I didn't want to, because I didn't know how things were or anything. No one explained them to me.

After that, I worked in a house as a maid. I worked in five or six houses and sometimes they treated me well, sometimes not. One lady didn't pay me. She still owes me twenty dollars. I worked taking care of her kids. Take them to school, wash the clothes, iron. She paid me ten dollars a week, that's what they used to pay. That was about 1970.

Then I met my husband. We met on a bridge crossing the Rio Grande. On Saturdays I would go to Matamoros to take money to my mother. On Sundays I would come back. I met him one time when I came back across.

We met in '71. We lasted for only a week and then we wanted to get married. We went to court and they told us that we couldn't get married because I was a minor. I was sixteen. They said my mother or my father had to come. So then, the brother-in-law of my husband, he went and got permission from immigration so that my mother could come and we could get married. See, my mother and father had much trouble to come here. Their birth certificates were burned during the revolution in Mexico, so they couldn't get the papers.

After my husband and I got married, we lived in Brownsville. Then we went to Wisconsin, to work in a factory for canning corn. For two weeks, they paid us $110, $115, each person. But we lived there only about a month because I started vomiting. They told me I couldn't stay because the doctor in the factory, he said I was in bad health. With my first child. I couldn't work anymore. So we left.

When we came back, my husband was work-

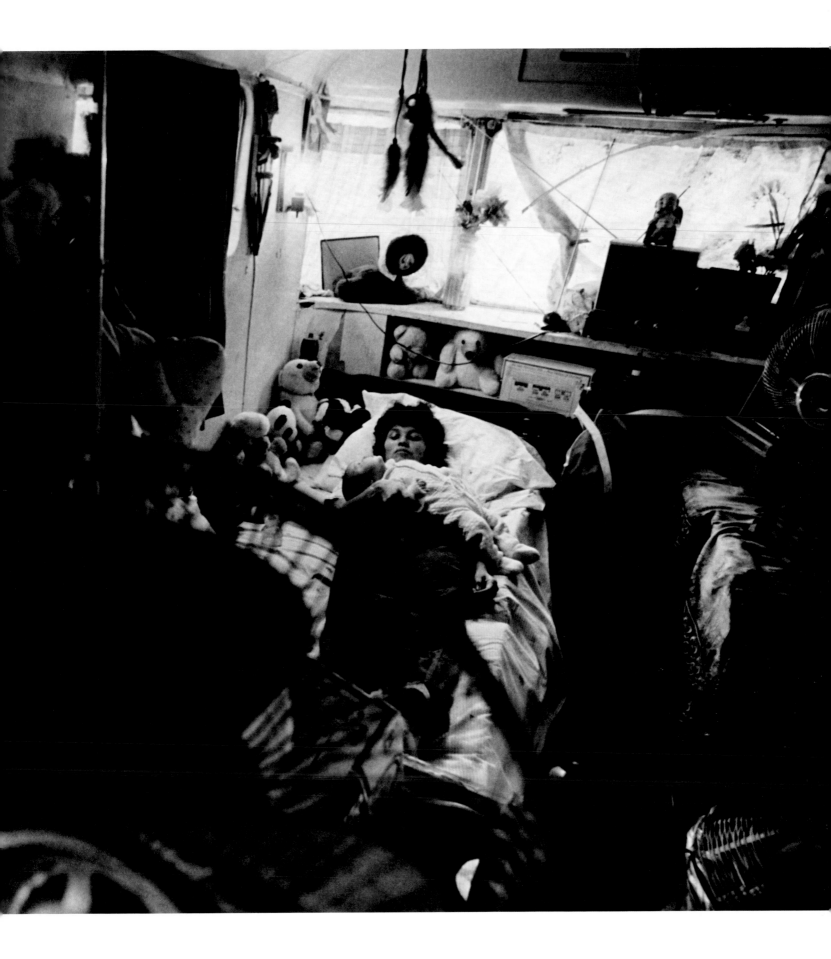

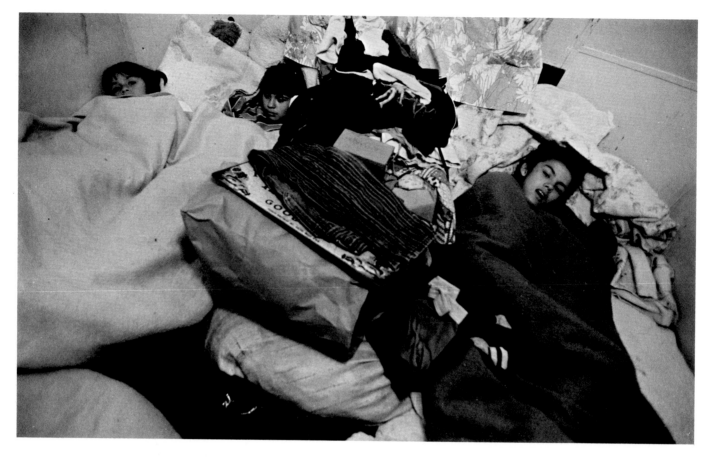

ing painting houses. It was hard. Sometimes he wouldn't earn anything all week and sometimes he earned $30, $40, $50. Sometimes he'd find something very good and earn $300 or $150 or $250. But then his brothers and nephews would help him work and after he gave to them, what was left?

I had the first baby with a doctor, with a clinic. It cost about $200 to $250. It was hard to pay. Next time, I had a midwife, in a house. It cost about fifty dollars. The third baby, the same. The fourth baby, the city clinic. They didn't charge me; Medicaid paid. With the fifth baby, I was sick. I had a tumor on the left side. At five weeks after the baby was born, they operated on me.

The tumor, it had much inside, hair and teeth. They say that when the tumor grows— that hair that is inside?—it can form cancer. But for me, they discovered it in time.

My husband went away. The twenty-third of October. He just left one day—he said, "I'll be right back," but he never came back. He was

lost about three or four days. I was waiting, crying, looking for him.

Then he called me on the telephone. He was in Houston. He had got arrested for transporting the illegals. He had to go to court. They found him guilty and he went on the bus to Big Springs, Texas, to the federal prison camp. They gave him, I think, ten years.

Before my husband went away, we never got the welfare. Now we get the welfare and the food stamps. Everything is expensive. When you buy, the food stamps, the money, it goes.

Also, we pay for the trailer—$160 a month. It's one room and it's crowded but it's better than a car. Because we slept in a car all during my pregnancy with Rosie, for six months. We parked on the side of the street, wherever we could. It was very cold. My husband slept in front with Ignacio. Tony and I slept behind. Tony was with me because he was small, and the girls, they were below on the floor.

We lost our house because the car broke down. My husband didn't want to leave it

'cause he thought the parts might get stolen, so he said let's sleep in the car. And while we were with the car and away from the house, our landlady who wanted us out took everything. Everything. Beds, all our clothes, a sewing machine. My husband didn't want to make trouble because I was pregnant again.

Later, we moved here to this trailer. It's much better here. The girls sleep on that bed by themselves by this side. And the boys sleep by themselves on the other side. The two little babies are with me. My husband slept on the sofa when he was here.

Many days now, we are waiting for my husband to come back. I think maybe he's coming here—to the jail in Brownsville—on the eighteenth. With the half moon. Then we can visit. He will stay in jail four more months, then they will let him go for good behavior.

We write to him many, many times. All the children write with a little letter and they all put the letters in one envelope. And Rosie, because she doesn't know how to write, she just puts her name, Rosie.

He writes many times too. I keep all his letters. This one, it came today:

Special, special wife,

Here I write you a few lines. With all my heart and respect, I hope that you are fine and also the children. Those are my sincerest wishes. As for me, do not worry. I am fine and with God's help, I will be with you all soon. That way I can start to work and help you all. Please pray to God so that I can get out soon.

Lola, I received the picture that you sent of the baby. She is very, very pretty. And fat. Give her a lot of kisses on my behalf. And the rest of the children, give them a big, big hug for me.

Take care of yourselves all of you. Say hello to Mama and to everybody. I love you with all my heart and I will never never forget you. Write to me fast please. Anything you want to write or as little as you want, but write to me. I love you.

(Translated from the Spanish)

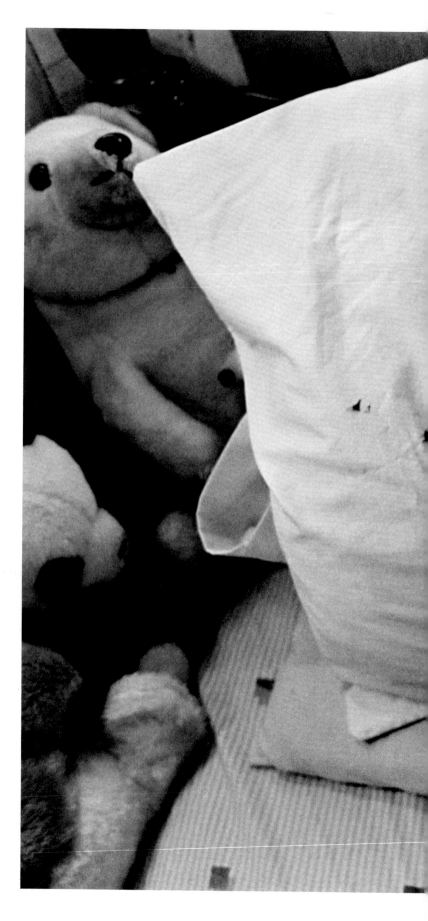

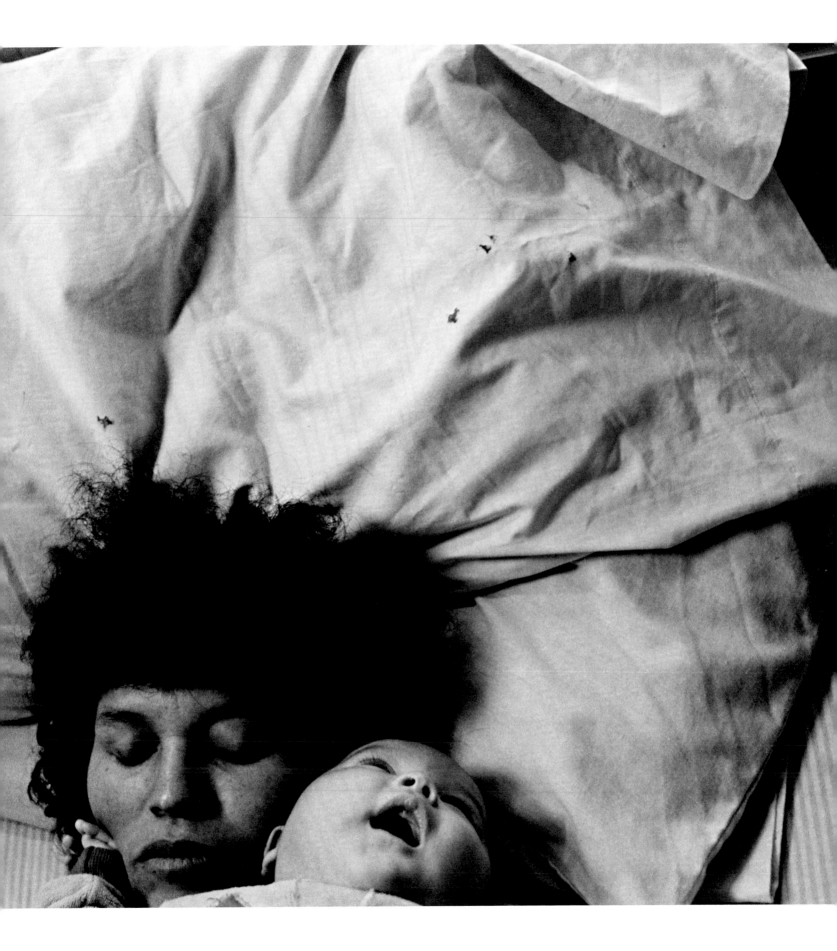

Afterword

When Consumers Union set out last year to document the face of poverty in America, hunger and homelessness had only just begun to reassert themselves in the American consciousness. This book was intended to be a bridge between the middle class—people like the millions of *Consumer Reports* readers—and their fellow consumers living below the poverty line.

It's possible for many of us to live our daily lives without ever encountering hungry or homeless people. In the Consumers Union lunchroom one day, I asked several of my suburban coworkers if they see people who are hungry or homeless. Many do not. Yet we must *see* them before we can care about them. And we must care about them before we are moved to end the intolerable conditions that mark their lives.

Ending intolerable conditions, after all, was an overriding concern of CU's founders. In the first issue of *Consumer Reports*, in 1936, they said that CU would not only test and give advice about products, but would join with others to help achieve the "decent standard of living" that seemed so unattainable during the Depression.

Today, more than fifty years since those words were penned, prosperity has replaced Depression for many Americans. Yet, in the midst of plenty, the number of hungry and homeless increases, and the national will to provide for that "decent standard of living" has not crystallized.

For fifty years, CU has probed and written about not only the high end of consumer needs—cars, appliances, and the latest symbols, VCRs and compact-disc players—but about the most basic consumer needs—food, housing, and health care. *Consumer Reports* has covered those subjects from the first issue. Today we cannot avert our journalistic eyes from the brutal fact that millions of Americans are living with those basic needs unmet or met so precariously that their very survival is threatened.

That brutal fact alone would be sufficient reason for CU to voice active concern about the poor consumer. But another reason has emerged on the economic landscape. Poverty is no longer the exclusive province of the so-called lower classes. An increasing number of middle class people, including the kind who subscribe to *Consumer Reports* or go to the library to read it, are slipping into poverty, too. Large-scale layoffs in major companies are adding to this army of involuntary recruits: unemployed professionals, white collar employees, and highly paid blue collar workers. Also increasing is the number of those employed at salaries so degradingly low that basic needs go unsatisfied. They join an unfortunately large group of people who have been poor for some time—albeit a "genteel poverty"—elderly widows and divorced mothers, for example.

Eugene Richards's camera and tape recorder found their way to only a handful of the approximately 35 million American people who live below the poverty line. The children we look at are among the 20 percent of all children who live in poverty. The black children under six we see are among the 50 percent of black children who live in poverty. (If we believed that being poor and being jobless are synonymous, we're wrong. More than one-sixth of the poor children, some 2.5 million, are in families where at least one parent works full time. More than 2 million people who work full time year round don't earn enough to escape poverty.)

This nation is reaping what we have sown. Cutbacks in federal spending for children and young adults, inflation without an increase in the minimum wage, reductions in unemployment benefits, an unemployment rate of over 7 percent (more than 8 million people), the emptying of mental institutions, cutbacks in public housing expenditures: all of these have caused this economic whirlwind.

And while Americans are a decent and generous people, largesse has not put food on the table or roofs over the heads of all who are without. The soup kitchens—a term resuscitated from the 1930s—can't do the job. Harvard's Physician Task Force on Hunger in America calls hunger a "growing epidemic."

And the U.S. Conference of Mayors has reported that in many cities surveyed, while demand for food assistance increased, the cities have had to turn away people in need.

Advocates for the homeless estimate that the number of homeless runs to the millions. The Mayors' Conference reported that there were an insufficient number of shelters and that homeless people have been turned away, too. Those are the facts that made a deep impression on us at Consumers Union.

The people whose words and photographs tell the stories in this book breathe a devastating meaning into facts and figures that might otherwise remain inert. This book is our attempt to take the wrapping off America's most unacceptable product—poverty—and to reveal what it looks like and feels like. We at Consumers Union remain committed to the mission with which we started—to help achieve a "decent standard of living" for everyone. We offer this book as part of that effort.

Rhoda H. Karpatkin
Executive Director
Consumers Union

Acknowledgments

Arkansas
Earl Anthes, Independent Community
Consultants, Inc.; Cherie Anthes, Arkansas
State Health Department; Will Golatt

California
Mumui Tatola, director, Tongan Community
Center; Paul Veamatahau, volunteer, Tongan
Community Center

Illinois
Linda Williamson, social worker

Massachusetts
Jerry Berndt, photographer; Sister Debbie
Chausee, Long Island Shelter for the Homeless

Michigan
Lucille Preston

Missouri
Beth Conway, writer/photographer

New Jersey
Mary Beach, social worker, Division of Welfare

New York
Randolph Scott-McLaughlin, lawyer, Center
for Constitutional Rights; Jerry Fox, social
worker

Pennsylvania
Jim Boon, lawyer, Florida Rural Legal
Services, Inc.; Marcia Spitz, social worker;
Anthony Cirillo, director of corporate
communications, Episcopal Hospital; Wayne
Woerner, farmer

South Dakota
Rich and Bonnie McBrayer, farmers; Val
Farmer, psychologist; Simon Zeller, social
worker; George Wellner, farmer; John and
Alice Schumaker, farmers; Barry and Lycel
Bennett, farmers

Tennessee
Marie Cirillo, founder, Rural Video, Inc.

Texas
Evelon Dale, executive director, Good
Neighbor Settlement House; Gracie Duvall,
volunteer, Good Neighbor Settlement House;
Rachel Torres, Brownsville Chamber of
Commerce; Margaret Robbins, U.S.
Commission on Civil Rights

Wyoming
Leann Carothers, Job Service of Wyoming;
Jeff Swainer; Judy Hoffman

I also wish to thank Susan Meiselas, Alice
Rose George, Margaret Sidlosky, David Spear,
Joe Rodriguez, Jim Lukoski, Maureen
Dowling, Paul Gauci, Catherine Chermayeff,
Ernie Lofblad, and Wendy Byrne for their
friendship and help.

E. R.

Eugene Richards is an award-winning Magnum photographer whose four previous books include *Few Comforts or Surprises: The Arkansas Delta* (1973), *Dorchester Days* (1978), *50 Hours* (1983), and *Exploding Into Life*, recipient of the Nikon Award for best photography book of 1986. He has received grants from the John Simon Guggenheim Foundation, the National Endowment for the Arts, and the W. Eugene Smith Foundation, and is the recipient of the 1987 International Center of Photography Journalism Award for "outstanding accomplishment in photographic reportage of the past year" for *Below the Line*.

Christiane Bird, the text editor, has a B.A. in literature from Yale University. Her stories have appeared in *Antaeus* and *Southern Review* and her articles have appeared in numerous national magazines. She is currently a staff writer at the New York *Daily News*.

Janine Altongy, story researcher, has a master's degree in social work from Columbia University. She has worked as a counselor for cancer patients and emotionally troubled children and as an outreach worker for welfare recipients.